Writers of Wales

D1461415

Editors
MEIC STEPHENS   R. BRINLEY JONES

M. Wynn Thomas

JOHN
ORMOND

University of Wales Press

Cardiff 1997

Foreword

This is a study of John Ormond the poet by one who did not know John Ormond the man. As such, it clearly has its limitations. Such excursions into the life as seemed to me inescapable, given the format of this series and the invitations issued by the poetry itself, are preliminary efforts only at constructing a rich narrative of an interesting and complex human being. That biographies can, at best, be but a narrative became intriguingly evident to me as I discussed John Ormond with those who did know him. After death (as also, perhaps, during life) a person is present to others primarily as story – a fact I have tried in places to register at the level of style, and something which I like to feel an old PICTURE POST hand would have understood. Every biography should perhaps be compelled to carry the subtitle: 'the story so far (and no further)'. And by 'story' I do not, of course, mean 'anecdote'.

My treatment of Ormond the film-maker is also relatively slight. Had not the series title, WRITERS OF WALES, persuaded me that my ignorance of film might in these circumstances be forgivable I should not have accepted the invitation to write this monograph. But even then, of course, forgiveness can only be partial, since Ormond the film-maker was an important aspect of Ormond the creative artist, and since Ormond the film-maker could sometimes be as significant a writer as Ormond the poet.

I accepted the invitation to prepare this study because I liked and respected such work by John Ormond as I had read. That liking and respect grew, rather than diminished, as I worked. And if the quality of his poetry is felt by some to have found a match (I would not venture to say found its match!) in the thoughtfulness and seriousness of my treatment of it, I shall be very well content, since that would mean that a useful step will have been taken in securing a continuation of interest in Ormond's life and work. That more than the makings of such an interest is already there is evident from the welcome inclusion of three of Ormond's poems (although not, in my opinion, his best) in the new (fourth) edition of THE NORTON ANTHOLOGY OF POETRY, that bible of the American university classroom.

I am immensely grateful for the help and encouragement I have received from all the people and sources listed below, but would emphasize that the opinions recorded here are solely and entirely my own. Glenys Ormond Thomas and Rian Evans have been particularly generous with their time and attention and have allowed me to scan the mass of as yet unsorted papers left by John Ormond; however, it goes without saying that what follows is not, except perhaps very occasionally and coincidentally, a reflection of their views. Of the many others who assisted me, I should like particularly to name the following: Dr Dannie Abse and Mrs Joan Abse, Mr Gilbert Bennett, Mrs Iris Cobbe, Professor Neil Corcoran, Mr Mick Felton, Mr Phil George, Professor Jeremy Hooker, Mr Chris Lawrence, Mr Colin Morris, Mr Tim Neale, Mr Selwyn Roderick, Dr Dai Smith and Mr Meic Stephens. In addition to granting me sabbatical leave to work on this study, University of Wales, Swansea provided me with valuable support through its library services. Equally important was the aid provided by the BBC Archive Library at Cardiff, Cambridge University Library and Swansea Public Library. And as always, my wife and my daughter supplied the kind of encouragement (and criticism) that is beyond price.

I

Dylan Thomas was born on a horseshoe bay. His friend, fellow townsman, and namesake, John Ormond Thomas, was born and raised in a horseshoe village – or so it seems today, if you drive from Killay to Gowerton. The road from nearby Swansea dips steeply down past the little terrace of cramped cottages where he was born, to enter the deep cwm formed when *the glacier long ago/ Gouged out the valley*. Crossing a stumpy bridge *with no grace*, over the *green/ Nothing* that was the railway track, it suddenly divides into two. While one road races straight on uphill, through that part of the village that lies in the direction of Three Crosses, the other turns abruptly right, past the row where Ormond's shoemaker father had his workshop, only to be thwarted in its progress by austere Ebenezer Chapel, gravely flanked by the hillside cemetery where the poet's dusty kinsfolk lie *In ones and twos and families*. Shamefacedly the road bends sharp right again, before belatedly reasserting itself and making directly for Gowerton. The figure this road thus makes of Dunvant is suggestive both of snug enclosure and of impending confinement, and as a maturing artist Ormond was to be at once deeply attached to his native village and yet ever watchful of its pinioning embrace. In the title of his fine Dunvant poem, 'Where Home Was', the past tense is a tell-tale sign both of continuing warmth and of sensible wariness – a wariness not only of the intimate claims of the place but also of the artistically disabling sentimentality to which it could give rise in him. It is a sentimentality that threatens to damage several of his poems about Dunvant.

John Ormond Thomas was born there in 1923. Dunvant was then a community close-knit to the point of clannishness; a small industrial hamlet nestled between the expanding (and soon-to-be encroaching) conurbation of Swansea, the large industrial townships of Gowerton and Gorseinon, and the beautiful open expanse of the Gower Peninsula. Although all three of those neighbouring areas left significant marks on his imagination, it was Dunvant that was the making of him both as man and as artist. In turn, he later remade the village in the image not only of his memories but of the geography of his own vision, when in 'Where Home Was' he saw it as a village in two halves, clamped together by bridges, *latchets of smooth/ Sandstone coupling the hills*. There the word 'coupling' and its cognates, neatly conjoin industry (railway trucks), fertility (sexual intercourse), camaraderie (couples), enduring community (*easier to let* [the bridges] *stand/ Than ever to pull them down*) and, of course, craft (as the bridges *mortised and clasped* two sides of the valley). Dunvant becomes a village born and bred of the union of contraries (as are life and art, in Ormond's conception). *How things summon their opposites*, he wrote in 'Blue Bath-gown', *Heat cold, togetherness apart*.

As many have noted, a lifetime's respect for his shoemaker father and the other artist-craftsmen of an industrial community lay behind Ormond's painstaking (and sometimes painsgiving) crafting of films and poems. In Dunvant, too, he first learned to

2

note the disregarded beauties hidden within apparent drabness, harshness and dereliction, a socially committed aesthetics that developed further during his formative years working with the cameramen of PICTURE POST, reaching its maturity in his lyrical documentaries of the sixties and the poetry of his middle age. In 'Where Home Was' he recalls not only the bridge as *a dingy/ Ochre hasp over the branch railway*, but also how *Nearby the sidings stretched in smells/ Of new pit-props leaking gold glue.* Unknown to himself, he was already seeing Dunvant, as a boy, with the prophetic eye of sensuous artistic appetite – the poem is unmistakably about the growth of a painterly poet's mind, even to the relishing of the contrast between dull brown and the sheen of silver when a penny is placed on the tracks to be flattened by a passing train.

Like Dylan Thomas (and many other writers) the young John Ormond was richly indulged, being an only child, often ill, living in the very bosom of a large extended family and in the midst of a readily knowable community. Kind relatives, reading aloud to him when he was housebound by rheumatic fever, helped kindle in him a lasting passion for books. His extended family on his mother's side (his father's family were outsiders from Merthyr, and Ormond himself was later in life a combination of insider and outsider) took on a further supportive role in his youth, since he was partly isolated from his Dunvant contemporaries by virtue of the fact that those born the other side of the Swansea town boundary, which was the bridge, attended nearby Gowerton County, while he travelled in the opposite direction, to distant Swansea Grammar School. Nurtured by the protective warmth of the family, and allowed an inner freedom, his imagination was licensed to go its own enthralled way, as he was to do, both as artist and to some extent as a man, throughout his life. Having absorbed emotional warmth early, he was thereafter able to radiate it in ways that attracted undoubted affection and sustained staunch friendships, even while his artistic demanding nature, flashes of dogmatism, emotional volatility and occasional irascibility – also perhaps a product of his early upbringing – could sometimes make for difficulties. Considerable freedom, underwritten by a close-knit family, with a strong central maternal presence, became a feature of both his personal and his artistic life. In PICTURE POST, and later at the BBC, he was a key member of an intimately small, talented team, and received fostering attention from Tom Hopkinson and Hywel Davies, just as he in turn was to further the careers of those who were apprenticed to him. He likewise enjoyed the relaxed camaraderie and conviviality of pubs such as the Wheatsheaf in London (which gave the youngster genial access to fellow writers and artists, such as W. S. Graham, Paul Potts, John Heath Stubbs and 'Richard Findlater'), and appreciated a similar milieu in Swansea (where his companions periodically included Dylan Thomas) and in pubs such as the Conway and Romilly in Cardiff.

Late in life, he found in the small Italian hillside town of Cortona, which became his spiritual second home, another Dunvant of sorts (its very church was dedicated, he wryly noted, to the patron saint of shoemakers) but with an antique grace, style and beauty to match its unaffected, welcoming friendliness. The beautiful film, FROM A TOWN IN TUSCANY, which he made about the neighbouring town of

4

Arezzo in the early sixties, made much of the fact that children there could be apprenticed to a craft, such as wood-carving, at the tender age of eleven. Thus Ormond emphasized that the great artists of the region – Petrarch, Michelangelo, Vasari and Piero della Francesca, whose paintings adorned the church – were not aristocrats but artisans of genius, craftsmen such as he had himself known as a boy. Like many of the villages on the western edge of the south Wales coalfield, Dunvant was less proletarianized than, say, the townships of the Rhondda. The older concept of the artisan still had validity in a community that retained aspects of rural society, and which readily respected the skills involved in the industrial process, particularly those of the tinplate workers who constituted a kind of industrial aristocracy throughout the Swansea hinterland. In the film, too, the singing of the Arezzo choir seemed to echo that of the celebrated Dunvant Male Voice Choir of his native village, when in his narrative he pointed out that these interpreters of the refined spiritual music of Palestrina were ordinary waiters, humdrum clerks, and factory workers.

Firmly grounded in Dunvant experience, an important part of John Ormond believed passion-ately in a democratic art that was the finest expression of collective social life. But another part of him, perhaps more ambiguous in its feelings about his early background, clearly saw the drawbacks in that idea. The inner debate between these two core aspects of his nature, a debate which powered much of his art and was conducted through it, is most evident in his Dunvant poem, 'Organist'. John Owen, market gardener-cum-organist, began as a perfectionist, sternly upholding the highest artistic standards, taking *no heed in the hymns/ Of the congregation trailing a phrase behind,/ Being intent and lost in the absolute beat.* Friends of Ormond speak of him, too, as sometimes oblivious to others, being obsessed, almost to the point of intolerance, with meeting the exacting demands of his art. But with the passing of the years, Johnny Owen became, in Ormond's characteristically witty phrase, *A Benthamite of music, he set more store/ By the greatest harmony of the greatest number.* When the congregation, inflamed by religious fervour, strayed enthusiastically off key, *John Owen would transpose/ By half a tone in the middle of the hymn/ To disguise the collective error.* Ormond here constructs an intelligently equivocal image of the role of the artist in the kind of Welsh democratic society from which he himself originated. Part of him admires the original uncompromising perfectionist in Johnny, and so regrets the later compromise, the abandoning of standards in the interests of serving the mass; but another part of him admires the sympathetic art with which Johnny tactfully changed key in order to give expression to the deepest collective emotions of his society. In the same way, later, Ormond was to be drawn both to PICTURE POST and to Ceri Richards; to the artistic loner, Vernon Watkins, and to the much more sociable genius of Gwyn Thomas. There was something of both in his own make-up, as is evident when he alternates in his mature poetry between a plain and a mannered way of writing.

Ebenezer, Capel yr Annibynwyr (Welsh Congregationalists), was the spiritual, social and cultural centre of Dunvant life. There, in the company of a throng of relations on his mother's side, Ormond worshipped as a boy, becoming a Christian pacifist in his youth. So numerous, indeed, was his mother's family that they were a choir unto themselves; his uncle Emlyn, trained by the father of the famous tenor, Walter Glyn, had an excellent voice. Ormond himself began his artistic career by performing in light operas and oratorios produced at the chapel. *What I am saying*, he wrote recalling this background, *is that I think I inherited a musical ear.* In due course, some of his poems were to seem like a continuation of music by other means. Even before leaving grammar school, he experimented with sonic patterns roughly based on Welsh *cynghanedd*, which, having only a chapel listener's knowledge of Welsh, he probably learned from Gerard Manley Hopkins.

It was also at morning service in Ebenezer Chapel that he had a Damascus experience which gave new birth to him as an artist. There he first saw the *straight-backed and lovely aloofness* of a genuine painter, a true non-conformist. *I am still astonished,* he wrote in 1984,

that Ceri [Richards] *should have emerged from Dunvant. All artists have to be born somewhere; but the exuberance and song of his drawing, the deep and searching colour, the lyricism and the solemnity of his themes seem so distant from a village dominated by the clenched moralities.*

Such astonishment ultimately found witty and suggestively ambiguous expression in his poem on 'The Birth of Venus at Aberystwyth', where the shockingly outré initial appearance of Venus at the local chapel (before she learns to *[wear] a safe beige hat for morning service*) seems distantly to recall the impact of Ceri Richards's wife, Frances, on the congregation of Ebenezer Chapel. That first glimpse of Richards, home from London on a visit, was for Ormond an instance of the way in which *chance governs so much at the forked roads of life*. Unexpectedly confirmed by that experience in his own burgeoning rebellion against the joylessness of the hymns that passed for art in chapel, he began symbolically to paint his way out of his horseshoe village by feverishly copying the straight vista of Hobbema's 'The Avenue, Middleharnis'.

His passion for art was not at this time nourished, as it was later, by visits to the pictures, although in middle age he did recollect the outrageously plush and blowzily baroque cinemas scattered throughout his drab working-class areas, and lovingly recited the litany of their exotic names: The Plaza, Rialto, Elysium, Castle, Albert Hall, Palace, Maxime, Tivoli. As a boy, he was able to get to the nearby Gowerton 'Tiv' only once a year, and even then had to leave early in order to catch the last bus home. In later life he turned this fact to good account by explaining

that until I was about twelve I never once saw the end *of any* single *film which accounts, I suppose, for my neurosis and my feeling that the world in general is an incomplete sort of place.*

(When not writing under the influence of one Thomas, he was sometimes in danger of being similarly charmed by the anecdotal genius of another (Gwyn).) As a boy, the future film-maker was not, then, an experienced picture-goer like his future friend, Dylan Thomas. Ironically, Ormond did not hear of Thomas at Swansea Grammar School, despite being briefly taught English by the poet's father. Excelling there as a runner, he was also encouraged by the school's art master in his aim of becoming an architect, but his wish to attend art school was implacably opposed by his mother. Instead, he went to the local University College of Swansea, but not before his whole life had been lastingly transfigured by his first passionate experience of poetry, in the form of Wilfred Owen's 'Exposure' and Dylan Thomas's 'The force that through the green fuse'.

He read both on the same night, in late April or early May, 1941, having that very day bought Denys Kilham Roberts's Penguin anthology, THE CENTURY'S POETRY, from the rehoused Morgan and Higgs bookshop in recently blitzed Swansea. Against the background of his savagely bombed city, he read first a sensuously anti-war poem, and then a poem which paradoxically affirmed the destruction that was the precondition and fate of all fertility. For a Christian pacifist this heady combination of circumstances was almost prophetically apt, virtually ensuring that over the subseqent decade John Ormond would become an eager participant in the Apocalyptic movement in the arts. That movement, also known as Neo-Romanticism, had in any case the strongest of ties with Wales, by virtue not only of the poetry of Dylan Thomas, Vernon Watkins, Keidrych Rhys, Lynette Roberts and the early Alun Lewis, but also of the work of artists such as David Jones, Ceri Richards (who lived and worked through the blitz in Cardiff), John Piper (based in north Wales) and Graham Sutherland, who was visited in Pembrokeshire by John Minton and John Craxton. Sooner or later, Ormond was to come into close creative contact with many of these figures.

He read both English and Philosophy at college (and

always admitted his debt to Thomas Taig, the drama specialist there); but it was the latter subject that really excited his imagination, thanks largely to the influence of Rush Rhees, a charismatic and intellectually austere American. The dedicated intensity of Rhees's thinking was utterly compelling and must have appealed to a student who remained instinctively attracted, throughout his life, to intellectual rigour. A close friend and favourite disciple of Wittgenstein's, Rhees regularly brought the great philosopher down to Swansea, where he readily mixed with the students, most of whom (like the future Welsh-language poet, Eirian Davies) were studying for the ministry. Ormond became a devotee of Wittgenstein's language philosophy, and, mediated through the bravura language games of Wallace Stevens's poems, this proved to be a significant influence on his mature work. Indeed, it was through Rhees's collection of modern American poetry that Ormond was first introduced to some of the masters of literary modernism, including Hart Crane (whose poem 'At Melville's Tomb' seems to inform sections of Ormond's youthful poem to Phil Tanner) and e. e. cummings. Studying philosophy also began to make him sceptical of the simplicities of Christian faith as he had known it. In many respects, Rhees put him into a discomfiting way of thinking that lasted an entire lifetime but that found adequate expression only in the hauntingly tentative syntax of a late poem like 'Castiglion Fiorentino'.

Ormond's training in the visual arts at this time was strictly extramural, in that he regularly visited the Glynn Vivian gallery, and surreptitiously attended drawing classes at the art school. His training as a writer was likewise largely extracurricular. His first published poem was entitled 'Collier'; a sidelong glance, perhaps, at Evan Walters's painting of that name, one of the youthful Ormond's Glynn Vivian favourites. A slight but graceful lyric, it was published in DAWN, the college literary magazine, in 1942.

> *There is no peace*
> *Within the collier's weird face,*
> *But a gaunt light*
> *Shoots in his eyes*
> *For knowledge of the earth*
> *Has made him wise.*
>
> *What is it worth*
> *This torrid knowledge of the earth?*
> *And darkness there*
> *Within his soul*
> *And each blue mark upon his face*
> *A ton of coal?*

The following year he contributed a prose sketch, 'Section From a Work in Progress' (apparently based on the death of his grandfather) and a poem, 'Bright Candle, My Soul'. The former, with its occasional Dylan-ish touches (*the biblical, mythical, parable mouth*), is closer to Caradoc Evans, in its lugubrious relish for the village grotesque, than any of his later writings about Dunvant. Central to this 'knowing' adolescent story (which has interesting connections with 'After the Funeral' which Ormond had recently read in THE MAP OF LOVE [1939]) is the fantasy of resurrecting his collier grandfather, whom he secretly views in his coffin, to represent the carpenter Christ in a modernized version of the Last Supper. Instead, stirred by seeing his own death prefigured in this corpse, he steals away to write a poem – as if, like the adolescent Dylan Thomas, he had discovered his deathly Muse. Of particular significance is the way in which the piece is both a tribute to his background and a rebellion against it – the speaker/artist lies to his mother (and Ormond, still living at home, was very close to his) about what he has seen and done. The impeccably obscure accompanying poem, apparently a challenge to face up to the harshness of life's underlying energy, has several fine phrases that sing out his talent. This talent was much more evident in the assured if imperfect sonnet, dedicated to Ceri Richards and published in the 1945 issue of DAWN, of which by then Ormond was English-language editor. Linking death and birth through the organicist metaphors already patented by Dylan Thomas in 'The force that through the green fuse', Ormond mirrored the anguished, oneiric style of painting to be seen in Richards's celebrated lithograph illustrations of that poem, issued by POETRY LONDON in 1947.

Helped, no doubt, by the poetry boom of the war years, Ormond actually became a London-published poet at the age of twenty, when in 1943 the Grey Walls Press published INDICATIONS, a small volume in which his poems appeared alongside those of two other young poets, James Kirkup and John Bayliss. The Press was known for its commitment to the New Romanticism, as defined in that period by a reviewer in the TIMES LITERARY SUPPLEMENT:

the apotheosis of romanticism, regarded as the utterance of the unconscious pouring through the shattered crust of the world which consciousness had previously defined with something of the irresistible necessity of a stream of lava.

The following year, Keidrych Rhys published three

poems by 'Ormond Thomas', flanked by contributions from Dylan Thomas and R. S. Thomas, in his Faber book of MODERN WELSH POETRY. In THE WELSH REVIEW, Ormond's contribution was praised by his then professor of English, W. D. Thomas (with whom the pacifist Ormond was at odds over the war), for its *sense of the mystery of things, the dream-like melancholy so-called Celtic passion . . . [and] an intimate sense communicated of a living universe.* Other poems published at that time in WALES, THE WELSH REVIEW, NEW ROAD and POETRY QUARTERLY brought him to the attention of Dylan Thomas and Vernon Watkins. It was the latter, home on leave from the RAF, who suggested that Ormond *ought not to publish any further collection until* [he] *was thirty,* a piece of advice on which he pondered for over five years, until eventually he *came to write less and to destroy nearly all of it.*

Watkins was critically astute. Having avidly absorbed Dylan Thomas and the poetry of other vatic Romantic vitalists such as Lawrence and Whitman, Ormond needed time to become truly himself as a poet. But although some of his early work was pastiche, it was talented pastiche. His ability to create beautifully burnished cadences was already apparent (*Sensations of the birth heat, softer/ than calm-brushed bracken in winter*), as was his taste for imperious conceptualizing. These were talents and traits he was never to lose. There were also early signs of his later gift for limpid accuracy, as in the opening of 'Poem in February', a Three Cliffs Bay poem amusingly dismissed by the reviewer in WALES as *further evidence for the view that we are a nation of beachcombers.* Perhaps coincidentally, it appeared in MODERN WELSH POETRY, alongside the

work of Dylan Thomas, just a year before the latter
published his superb 'Poem in October':

> *Walking besides the lank sea-shore in February,*
> *with the faint birdmarks, triangular,*
> *and the grave curve and cry of the whirlpool bay,*
>
> *I set a line the wave cannot destroy,*
> *wave turning upon the dunes, beyond the rock*
> *first searched and sought out by the renewing tide*
> *that leaves no hidden sanctuary.*

('Poem in February')

This deft kind of writing may well have appealed to
Tom Hopkinson, who hired Ormond as a PICTURE
POST journalist, virtually straight from college
(except for a month on the BRENTWOOD GAZETTE), on
the strength of the poems that accompanied his
application for the job. Hopkinson, who had himself
published a short story in HORIZON, was at that time
hoping to staff the post-war POST with maverick
young talents from unorthodox, non-journalistic
backgrounds. (Another recruit, for example, was
Robert Kee.) Since its first sensational impact in 1939,
the POST, with sales consistently topping the million,
had developed into a national institution. Described
by Hopkinson as deliberately *provocative and contro-
versial*, the paper had throughout the war proved not
only the vast attraction of enterprising photographic
journalism but also its immense potential as enter-
tainment, as a form of popular education and as a
way of reflecting society so that society was stimu-
lated to reflect on itself. Anticipating that for Britain
the post-war years would be a time for *recovering,
taking stock, and trying to adapt itself to its new position
in the world*, Hopkinson was looking, in 1945, for

staff who shared his crusading, leftward-inclining zeal for radical social change. While determined to consolidate the paper's wartime reputation for gritty, uncompromising and radically egalitarian portrayals of life, Hopkinson also shared the view of the high-minded centre-left that *the ballet is as natural a source of enjoyment as Manchester United*. (Years later, Ormond, still loyal to this ideal of quality education in the arts for all, used to remark that his films of writers and artists were designed to appeal to *intelligent sixteen year olds*.) As editor, Hopkinson allowed his reporters an exhilarating degree of freedom to initiate and implement ideas, but always insisted that priority should be given to the needs of the brilliant photographers (such as Bert Hardy and Bill Brandt, who was very much attuned to the New Romantic movement in the visual arts), whose work was the pride of the paper as well as the basis of its mass appeal. Indeed, so indulgent was Hopkinson's way of handling his photographers that an indignant colleague once splutteringly protested: *You treat the cameramen of this paper like . . . like . . . Royal Children!*

For Ormond the writer and future film-maker the period of work on the POST (1946–9) in tandem with cameramen was probably the most profoundly educative of his life. He learned to make words complement images, rather than repeating or competing with them; he learned to write arresting but not patronizing captions; he learned to think like a camera; and he learned to write with a deftness of touch and a simplicity that was not simplistic. As a cocky but no doubt rather callow youngster, he also clearly revelled in the company of what Hopkinson described as *a talented, individualistic, somewhat hard-boiled group of journalists, distrustful of authority, not apt to accept slogans or to swallow without examination the assumptions of power politics. So far as it had a common political alignment, this would be left, though not very far left, of centre.*

As he began to develop professionally, Ormond's private life was blossoming too during this period. Although he had met his future wife, Glenys, during his first year at college – she came from the village of Loughor, a mere two miles or so from Dunvant – he began to court her only in his final year. He married her in the following year, 1946; it was to prove a valuable lifelong partnership.

The whole ethos of PICTURE POST was permissive and it encouraged and enabled Ormond to pursue his own creative vision after a fashion. So, for instance, his instinctive feeling for the elegiac found expression in a piece on a coster's funeral. Its evocative description of that rare relic, an elaborately ornate horse-drawn hearse, is redolent of regret for the passing not of a person but of a whole era of London history, focused in the image of the ostler blackening *the* [horses'] *hooves with a brush he dipped in a pot of tarry substance.* Then, via a deeply felt tribute to the dignity that working people can exhibit as much in the face of death as in facing up to life, the piece turns into an impassioned defence of the new National Insurance scheme that would ensure adequate coverage of funeral costs, regardless of the social class of the deceased. The same sympathy for the underdog emerges in a documentary essay on a gutsy group of people struggling to run a youth centre for Liverpool's street children. What is interesting is that Ormond already demonstrates a capacity to alternate, according to the occasion, between consciously fine and finely tuned writing and straight reportage, where he deliberately effaces himself stylistically, placing himself entirely at the service of his subject. This sensitive adaptive capacity was to be a prominent strength of his as a film-maker.

For an example of fine writing, one could not ask for better than his strikingly filmic account of the dis-interment of Yeats's body. Ormond witnessed the raising of the body from a cemetery in the south of France and its return for burial in Sligo:

At seven o'clock on a September morning, the sexton climbed the path to the cemetery, laid his coat outside the tiny graveyard chapel of St Pancras and began clicking with a hoe at the odd, inch-high weeds around the tomb-stones before the building. Photographs of the French and Italian dead buried around smiled, stared, happy or sullen, from their marble memorials. On the far side of the cemetery wall, in the clear morning sun and silence, a grasshopper rasped a coarse monotone where the hill pitched to an olive-grove below. Nothing seems more remote than the bleak stone walls, the tints and hints of autumn and the feathery rain that waited on the west coast of Ireland.

This atmospheric opening 'shot' – its subject left cunningly undisclosed – effectively turns the accompanying photographs into moving pictures, by embedding them in a visualized narrative. The artfulness of the writing carries the essay through to a plangent conclusion:

It was six in the morning and dark when she started into Galway eleven days later, and grey dawn as she slowed, approaching the first light of land. The welcoming crowd and the gulls stood out black against her prow. The wind behind her was full of rain.

17

Many of Ormond's contributions to the POST were not signed, but of those that were some of the best were about Wales, including an investigative report on a protest against the great tracts of upland still in the tenacious grasp of the War Department. A profile of the old Gower folk-singer, Phil Tanner, is interesting to read alongside the poem Ormond wrote about him at about the same time, and again the tone is predominantly reminiscent and elegiac. Even a quirky piece about the topiary of David Davies, who had recently died after years of snipping images of Biblical events and personages out of privet, ends by darkening into elegy: his son-in-law

sometimes despairs: for he is the last man to claim the kind of Biblical knowledge which belonged to his father-in-law, and in whom it was joined with an unending fastidious patience.

But Ormond's most sustained and compelling tribute to that dying, Dunvant-recalling breed, the Welsh industrial craftsman, is to be found in his magnificent portrait of Blaenau Ffestiniog, 'Slate Town'. Remarkably enough, considering its high quality, it was the very first picture-essay he completed for PICTURE POST, and it strikingly anticipates aspects not only of his later Dunvant poems but also of one of his earliest, and best, films, ONCE THERE WAS A TIME (1961), which eavesdrops on the talk of two old Rhondda miners. His essay celebrates the cultural richness of a society represented by the figure of Moelwyn Jones, who *splits slates for a living, but as an Eisteddfod bard lives for poetry,* and it concludes with a translation by Ormond of one of Jones's poems. The profile of the town is brilliantly caught by the accompanying photographs, including one of squat, gaunt, 'terraces' of slate tombstones, black against the light, with one weakling – its edges gouged by the weather – leaning slightly forward, emphasizing the stern enduring uprightness of all the others. And the assignment gave Ormond what was, perhaps, his first opportunity to venture underground – into the slate equivalent of the Dunvant seam. *Deep in the mountains,* he wrote,

a thin stream runs down through the walls of the mine. It washes the slate and the slag, but no one will ever know whether it makes them clean. How long it has run that way no one can ever tell you. They only know that it falls down through the levels, softening the grey mud patterned by the miners' boots, rusting the rails which curl away into the hill, under the hanging roof.

Above ground, he turns the slatescape of industrial waste into a Kyffin Williams-like landscape:

As we climbed, the huge tips of slate rubble seemed to raise themselves from their sullen, one-coloured sprawling down to the town, until their outline grew sharp and jagged against the sky

– a land against the light, to borrow the very title of his later film on Williams's work.

Of the POST's reporters, it was Ormond who usually wrote about artists, exhibiting as he did that extraordinary sensitivity to the inscape of their art, and fascinated comprehension of the techniques involved, that characterized his fine later films on poets and painters. He could evoke a singer's ability to sensualize the world through sound: *Her songs are, of course, revue songs that go down like stones dropped into a well; but they land like feathers and without touching the sides.* But he also pinpointed the *means* by which she achieved her effects:

She sets her voice to a tone which is immediately, and without further ado of having to get to grips with the song, as clear as distilled water. She hits her words alive in the middle, but coaxingly, and though coaxingly, with none of the croon and hum that is typical of the singing voice of her race.

Ormond's own life as a poet during this period was largely confined to the Soho pubs, where journalism literally rubbed shoulders with the London bohemia of the day. There he met Neo-Romantic poets and artists such as John Minton, the two Roberts (Colqhoun and MacBryde), George Barker and of course Dylan Thomas, who had connections with the world of film, as had others whom Ormond met at that time. His developing friendship with Thomas enabled the Post to feature him in 1946 and to publish his 'Conversation about Christmas' in 1947. Unlike Thomas, however, Ormond enjoyed a warmly secure and unfailingly supportive home life, to which he paid tribute in his early poems first to his daughter and then later to his son. Belonging as they do to a notable genre, stretching from Coleridge to Thomas and Watkins, these poems are magic verbal spells, rapt incantations to ward off the evil powers hovering over a slumbering baby (*And so, my midnight listener, wild owl call/ Blind for carrion, with the long dead fall/ Unravelling leaves, haunts the October wood*). Full as 'Midwinternight' is of elusive echoes of Dylan Thomas and other poets – Yeats's 'Prayer for my Daughter' most obviously, but also Eliot's 'Rhapsody on a Windy Night' – it nevertheless generates fine sonorities of its own. In so strenuously striving to imagine (and imaginatively to *will*) a protected existence for the baby amidst the mad ragings of life's weather, Ormond also gives touching expression to a 'new' father's sense of the vulnerability not only of his daughter but also, through her, of himself. In his hyperbolic evocation of the world of childhood as pastoral idyll, he recalls the post-war Dylan Thomas of 'Fern Hill', whose rhythms set the tempo of Ormond's own: *The time that is always with her/ Waits for her eyes to awake and raise up/ The sun that is kind from its dark.*

These poems are reminders that the relationship between the poet and the journalist in Ormond was one of opposites as much as of continuities and complementarities. Whereas the journalist could go with the flow of language, the poet (as Ormond later remarked) frequently had to work against that facile flow, looking always for the undertow. It was his desire to progress as a poet (allied to his disillusionment with commuting and hankerings after south Wales) that caused him in 1949 to announce to his startled wife that he had already (impetuously, and without consulting her) taken up the longstanding offer by the editor of the SOUTH WALES EVENING POST (Dylan Thomas's old paper) of a job in Swansea whenever he wanted it. It turned out to be an unwise and unhappy move, redeemed only by the congenial times to be had in the company of the Swansea set of artists – Fred Janes, Daniel Jones, Vernon Watkins and Dylan Thomas during his periodic visits home from Laugharne.

II

At the EVENING POST Ormond acted as sub-editor, occasionally writing a review of a book that took his fancy and sometimes contributing items of topical interest to TIME-LIFE magazine. His review in the EVENING POST of Dylan Thomas's COLLECTED POEMS is intelligent but undistinguished (although Thomas seems to have liked it). More interesting, oddly enough, is his report on a local camera club exhibition, where he politely criticizes the stiffness of the photos (getting his subjects to relax was to be a cardinal aim as a film-maker), lectures photographers on the camera's power to *reveal the reasons that underlie social and natural phenomena* (a lesson which he had learnt at the PICTURE POST and was later to put to good use), calls for photos that explore the *lapse of time* (as he was signally to do in BORROWED PASTURE), and singles out a picture of the wreck of the Santampa for special praise:

it gives *the whole evil of the sea . . . It is a document – not merely of the particular incident, but of the cruelty of water and the dynamite in the frills and flounces of the pretty, sugary, white-lace waves that move so gently through some of the other photographs.*

In that description one recognizes Ormond's own fascination with what, in the review of Dylan Thomas, he had called the *basic forces of decay, war, violence, Time, death, unkindness, lack of charity – and love.* Against these, he said, Thomas had built his *ark of words* – as, indeed, Ormond himself had done for his daughter in 'Midwinternight'.

Ormond was fond of telling his small children stories and in November, 1952 he turned his hand to writing one for the EVENING POST. The resulting tale proved to be incidentally expressive of his own chronic need for the arts of language. Johnny the Giant, mayor of Tumbledown town, starts to gabble incomprehensibly backwards after accidentally breaking the tiny mechanical bird made of precious metals which would serenade him to sleep every night. He is cured only when he manages to teach a real bird to sing to him in its stead. At this time Ormond was experiencing difficulties with his own 'song'. His speed of writing, and his productivity rate (both remarkably high during his college days) had slackened noticeably during his period with PICTURE POST and it scarcely improved at Swansea. But he did attempt to find more time for his own writing, and his EVENING POST years resulted in two significant and strikingly contrasting poems, as well as 'No Room at the Inn', a poetic drama commissioned by the BBC.

Ormond's homecoming was, like Dylan Thomas's 'Return Journey' (which Ormond later filmed), to a Swansea the old heart and character of which had been shattered by the 1941 bombing. 'City in Fire and Snow' was his attempt to come to terms both with that devastation and with the post-war threat posed by the H-bomb. An ambitiously orchestrated poem written in a febrile style, it is an uneasy combination of secularized ritual based on Thomas's 'Ceremony After a Fire Raid' (*Angelus bells for ritual frost begin/ Their clear call for service*) and the kind of Dante-esque converse with spirits to be found in

Eliot's wartime 'Little Gidding' (a beckoning figure is pursued *Through the arcaded gardens of inferno*). However, the poem – centring as it does on symbolic murder – is closer to Grand Guignol (or to the cruder kinds of thirties Expressionist cinema) than to Dante. A symbolist phantasmagoria, it is essentially structured around a female figure representing snow (the cold peace to be found in the oblivion of death) and a male figure representing fire (the agony through which we pass to death). There are moments of undeniable power, as when the attraction of snow is set not against fire but against the callously torrential energy of life, streaming through the heart and falling *oblivious in a cataract/ White with fear yet hurling down/ Drawn by it knows not what*. In general, though, the poem is interesting less in its own right than as a belated and rather benighted example of forties Apocalyptic art. Commenting on the work produced by Ceri Richards around the time of the Cardiff blitz, the critic David Mellors has recalled the contemporary words of another Neo-Romantic artist, Cecil Collins:

The sky of our time has been lit from the beginning of childhood by the light of the Apocalypse, always before our eyes have ridden the Four Horsemen. Such a light is therefore the light of my pictures.

'City in Fire and Snow' is an important reminder that Ormond's discovery of poetry had been intimately connected with the devastating air raids on Swansea. His lifelong belief in the humanizing power of the artistic imagination (as preached by such key wartime journals as HORIZON and POETRY LONDON) owed more than a little to those desperate initiating circumstances.

If his elegy for a city is the grandiose apotheosis of his early style, then 'My Dusty Kinsfolk' is the first of his real Dunvant poems, and the first substantial indication of his mature style. It was written sometime after the death of his father in 1950, although uncertainty remains about exactly when the poem was completed in its published form. The wry, arch opening, *My dusty kinsfolk in the hill,/ Screwed up in elm*, alerts the reader to the complexity of meanings and emotions to come, while also signalling a self-protective distancing of the poet from the charged emotions naturally involved in this fond yet perilous claiming of acquaintance with his dead relatives. Thus protected, he is able to risk the moving familiarity of tone that follows, while never wholly dropping his talismanic dryness of manner. He continues to equivocate to the end, even punning disturbingly on sounds ('yew/you') in the concluding lines. The whole poem is permeated by doubleness of feeling quietly realized at the level of sound and phrasing. Not only is it both requiem and celebration, it is also both invocation and exorcism – he at once invites haunting and deeply fears it, and he feels with and for the dead while wishing to ward off the death they threaten to visit on himself. It is a remarkably fine poem, unmistakably his own, and yet he seems to have lacked the confidence at the time to base a whole new style upon it.

Ormond was still working on the EVENING POST when in 1953 it carried the story of Dylan Thomas's death and funeral. It was a loss that devastated him personally and as an artist. It was also an event signalling the end of the Neo-Romantic era, and the new trends in British (and in American) poetry, already well under way, were deeply uncongenial to one of Ormond's temperament. *The coming Movement,* as Andrew Crozier has written, *held Thomas in particular disrepute and gave the impression that it thought his premature death a deserved consequence of a lifestyle and poetic style combined.* Forty years after the event, this whole Movement attitude was memorably enshrined in the sneering account in Kingsley Amis's MEMOIRS of Thomas's visit to the English Society at University College, Swansea. The anecdote includes a cameo of *a Welsh poet of small eminence by the name of John Ormond Thomas,* who was depicted as a Thomas groupie. It is as if the English Movement poets had literally invaded Ormond's own space, and place – an impression reinforced by the simultaneous appearance in University College, Swansea's literary magazine DAWN (1950) of both Ormond the former student's 'Midwinternight' and Amis the new English lecturer's Movement-style poem on Swansea Bay.

The virtual abandonment of poetry by Ormond from the mid-fifties was no doubt in large part due to pressure of work and the alternative creative possibilities offered by film. Also significant, however, was the ending (symbolized by Dylan Thomas's death) of the social and artistic conditions that had made his early poetic style possible and meaningful. And although he had already, in 'My Dusty Kinsfolk', effectively evolved a new kind of poetry, that too, with its singing lines surcharged with strong emotion, was far too obviously derived from forties Romanticism ever to pass for fifties poetry – whether that of the Movement, or (slightly later) that of the British counterparts of the American Objectivists and Confessionals.

His journalistic experience (and such radio work as

he had also sporadically been doing) stood him in good stead in 1955 when he was taken on by the BBC in Cardiff as *the* Television News Assistant, that is the one and only one, at a time when *There was no Cardiff studio, no news cameras, no film, no (as the saying goes) nothing*. This in effect meant that he was responsible for setting up television news in Wales. His adventures with the Outside Broadcast Unit, tramping Wales in search of film footage for insertion in both English-language bulletins (from London) and Welsh-language bulletins (from Cardiff) were entertainingly recalled, decades later, in a radio essay. His regular trips to London (where the bulk of the editing work was done) taught him that people there referred to TELENEWYDDION as 'Radio Look-you'. Back in Cardiff, working out of *a small vestry cupboard of a studio*, he found *the sole means* [he] *had of communicating with the London telecine engineers* [during a live broadcast] *to get them to run the next film was a field-telephone that was clearly a relic of trench warfare*. Ormond was understandably pleased when, in 1957, he was chosen to head a new full-time documentary film unit of eight people, equipped with new cameras and editing machines.

A SORT OF WELCOME TO SPRING, the first film produced by the unit (another of whose responsibilities was to supply news stories), was based on further experience gained by Ormond before and during his move from Swansea. In 1955 his old PICTURE POST editor, Tom Hopkinson, by then literary editor of the NEWS CHRONICLE, invited him to write a weekly verse caption for the 'Saturday Picture', the photograph highlighted on the features page of the paper. For the most part this resulted in light verse, deliberately occasional in character, popular in idiom and sentiment, topical in tone, fluently rhyming in predictable couplets. But it was an eight-month exercise (regretfully terminated by Hopkinson for financial reasons) that reinforced Ormond's Picture Post habit of writing to a visual image and encouraged in him a new dexterity and flexibility of poetic expression. And when, occasionally, a picture would really reverberate through his imagination, the result was not resourcefully pliant verse but compelling poetry. An example can be found in the concluding lines on a 'Daffodil in Snow': *Here, in a while, the galaxy will dwindle/ To nothing and its melting death rekindle/ New fire from dark to set the sun at once/ Ablaze upon its new impermanence.* And the whole of the poem appended to a picture of squabbling seagulls is masterly:

> *Startled and startling whiteness. White of wing,*
> *As white of snow above the morning tide.*
> *Whiteness as white of waves just toppling:*
> *White crest, white feather, shaded underside.*
> *The war of flight. Neutrality's restraint*
> *From early sunlight mustering new brightness.*
> *Instant of new possession, new complaint.*
> *Instant of whiteness overtaking whiteness.*

In one sense this is Vernon Watkins ('Music of Colours') superimposed on Dafydd ap Gwilym. But it is also unmistakably an anticipation of Ormond's characteristic later device, used in many poems from 'Definition of a Waterfall' to 'Certain Questions for Monsieur Renoir', of silhouetting the otherwise ungraspable essence of a phenomenon by outlining it with conceits (rather as a knife-thrower carves out the shape of a living target which remains untouched). It therefore seems appropriate that these News Chronicle verses should apparently be the first to carry his new signature, 'John Ormond', an identification mark which he had been persuaded to adopt by the Head of Programmes, Hywel Davies, aware as he was of the confusing plethora of Thomases (not to mention Davieses!) at the BBC. (His dropping of the Thomas may also, of course, have been a subconscious attempt to provide himself with an identity, as a creative artist, wholly separate from that of Dylan.) Imposingly different though it sounded, the name 'Ormond' had actually been purloined by the Dunvant station-master from Derry Ormond (a station near Strata Florida) as a name for his son, and was thence again borrowed by Ormond's mother. (A private fact that lends further piquancy to the well-known Ormond poem, 'Lament for a Leg'!) Such a family joke must have appealed to a man celebrated for his love of verbal humour, practical jokes and inventive anecdotes. In one not insignificant sense, poetry itself was for him an incorrigible play with words – he took great pleasure, late in life, in pointing out that in 'Homing Pigeons' he had *used the syllables of the Welsh word for 'shepherd' ('bugail') in the word 'beguilement', and put it against 'shepherds'*, in the line *What beguilement shepherds the heart home?*

It was as John Ormond that he wrote and produced A Sort of Welcome to Spring (1958), a notable film which owed something to his interest in the Opies' famous book on the rhymes and lore of school-children. The film was closely based on the successful format of pictures accompanied by verse commentary to which he had worked at the News Chronicle – except that the images were in this case moving pictures and the verse commentary (again mostly in rhyming couplets) was extensive. As always, and as befitted an old PICTURE POST hand, Ormond avoided what is known to professionals as the Lord Privy Seal tendency – that is he avoided repeating in images what the words literally signified (a lord, a privy, a seal . . .). Instead his exquisite verse worked as elaborate descant to the camera's music, and was written in a deft, unobtrusive, yet intricately thoughtful style which both contrasted with the clotted intensities of Ormond's early poetry and anticipated something of the graceful ease and complexity of his mature manner.

The evocative counterpointing of word and image is again a key feature of ONCE THERE WAS A TIME (1961), a wonderful documentary portrait of the remarkable society of the Rhondda in its twilight years. The words are entirely those of two old miners, William Thomas and Teify Jones, as they companionably indulge in a lifetime's habit of friendly argument and reminiscence, producing as they do a vivid sense – comic and serious by turns, but always unfailingly impressive – of the past they have known and the history (including a world war) which they have served in. The Marxist William, a sharp-voiced and sharp-witted atheist whose incisive views dominate the opening of the film, hones his rational materialism against the rather self-satisfied pieties of Teify, whose orotund pulpit cadences are in keeping with the comfortable plumpness of his body. And as these two spellbindingly talk, the camera does some visual eavesdropping on its own account, wandering at large around them, snooping through the valley streets, watching the silent domino-players listlessly killing time in the club, noting the vast collection of unconsulted books on improving subjects in the miners' library, joining the sparse chapel congregation at its mournful hymn-singing, capturing the catatonic faces of old people marooned in the present, whose features are as hauntedly still as the photographs that adorn their old-fashioned mantelpieces. Such images, multiplied apparently at random, interact unpredictably and tangentially with the ongoing dialogue, so that for instance William's opening reflections on the origins of civilization in the river valleys of the fertile crescent (both miners are formidably well-read, and can quote Shakespeare, Hume and Kipling seemingly at will) are accompanied by grey shots of coal-trucks in bare colliery sidings.

Empathetic portraiture, a desolating evocation of social displacement, an affectionate tribute to survivors' courage, and a lyrical treatment of harshly beautiful landscape – these striking features of ONCE THERE WAS A TIME were also some of the stylistic and interpretative qualities that had helped make BORROWED PASTURE, Ormond's landmark documentary, such an outstanding critical and popular success a year earlier in 1960. That film – a portrait that grew out of an original intention to capture the life of the expatriate Polish community in post-war Wales – showed two former soldiers from Poland, with heavily etched faces, stranded in a strange land after an epic trek across wartime Europe, and poignantly struggling to farm in the Lampeter area. It had a strong narrative line, created both through pictures, by rhythmically imaging the different phases of the changing year and through the words of Ormond's beautifully phrased, yet self-effacingly attentive commentary, which employed blank verse and occasional internal rhyme:

This is the simple story of two men
Who came upon a stubborn piece of land
That lay neglected for a generation.
Here, in despair, but hoping in their hands,
They worked together and, as best they could,
Borrowed rough pasture from the alien ground and water
And coaxed small comfort from decrepitude.

This is poetry reminiscent of Robert Frost's NORTH OF BOSTON, and which anticipates Ormond's mature style. Recalling that description of the farmers as men *hoping in their hands,* he later explained that it

had come from that chapter in the Apocrypha which praises the smiths and labourers of this world and gives them their place though 'they do not sit in the seats of the mighty'.

The connection with his Dunvant past is movingly clear. Reinforcing both words and pictures, and turning the whole film into a tone poem, was the music specially composed by Arwel Hughes, and based on folk songs which Ormond had carefully collected from expatriate Poles living in Pembroke-shire. (He always took great trouble over the music for his films, listening for hours to lesser known music by Janacek, Hindemith, Francaix, etc.) However dated or self-consciously arty BORROWED PASTURE may seem to present viewers used to *cinéma-vérité* techniques or a fly-on-the-wall approach to documentary, it remains a masterly composition in the romantic-realist style pioneered in the classic work of Flaherty and Grierson during the thirties, and perfectly illustrates what attracted Ormond to the medium:

In the new unit a number of things I was committed to could come together: my social concerns, my involvement with the

graphic (I had always been a keen cinema-goer), my writing and
my love of music.

Time (in both its human and its natural aspects) is in
many ways the subject of this film, which itself took
more than two years to make; Ormond later recalled
the process of working *to get the mood and the spirit of*
that forbidding place, and the fortitude, both physical and
emotional, of these men who, now trusting us, became our
friends. That friendship long outlasted the making of
the film, and through the good offices of the Lord
Chancellor, Elwyn Jones (a native of Llanelli), Ormond
was able to bring Vlodek's wife from Poland. Public
response to BORROWED PASTURE – viewers sent in
money; MPs asked questions in the House – was a
tribute to the powerfully simple human appeal of a
film that had been intricately crafted. Before shooting,
Ormond made extensive preliminary drawings and
sketches that are still extant. (*This needs good clouds* he
notes at one point.) Later he graphically recalled the
visual materials with which he had worked –

a bending, ragged lane, ankle-deep in mire; . . . a broad, fast-
running stream, now swollen to a river and across a flimsy
bridge of bits of branches and broken boxes. On the bank above
stood an old house in terrible decay, great holes gaping in the
roof, its domain 65 sullen and sour acres.

There, over the months, they

filmed the day's routine, the repairing of the roof with slates
from an abandoned pigsty; a snowfall; the endless grind, the
draining of the days; the priest's celebration of the Mass, the
consecration of the Wine and the triumphant raising of the Host
in the grey, stone kitchen. As the great wheel and the seasons
slowly turned we filmed the ritual and the Mass of Life.

33

After twelve years in this hermitary, Ormond recalled, the two men still addressed each other as 'Mr': *Only in two shots in the film I was to make were they seen together, this to mirror their isolation.* [Vlodek] *Bulaj had perhaps fifty words of English, Okolowicz none* – a point the significance of which is memorably brought out when Vlodek stumblingly fails to make himself understood by an increasingly impatient telephone operator. Yet during his months there Ormond heard *two fragments of speech* by Vlodek which he treasured and eventually had him repeat on camera: *As the last music faded his words gave the film its fading fall: 'What is life? you know, it is trouble. Without trouble, you know, life it is pleasure, it is too easy. But it is not life.* And: *'You know, without the farm I am nothing. I am the farm and, you know, the farm it is me.'* Thus ended a film *which had become an obsession* and which is so exactly true to Ormond's credo as a film-maker:

All true documentary has to have an element of revelation: that of the camera in a place as proxy witness for the audience; of a complex circumstance revealed in a simple and understandable form; of people and things in a seemingly ordinary workaday world poetically revealed, inductive rather than deductive at heart, moving from particular observation to general, universal conclusion.

Such a vision of film was consistent with that of René Clair, whose prophetic comments Ormond appreciatively recorded at this time in his notebook:

The only poetry that can exist in a film is the poetry created by the shot itself. It is a singularly new poetry, the rules of which have not yet been established . . .

Cinematographic poetry springs from visual rhythms . . .

34

[films] have proved that the spectators' interest can be sustained for a long time without the help of a contrived plot. The image suffices. Who knows? Perhaps the day will come when a mere succession of shots with no definable link between them, united only by a secret harmony, will excite an emotion similar to that which comes from music.

On seeing BORROWED PASTURE the old maestro John Grierson, though unaware that Ormond was a writer, declared him to be a poet, and later arranged for him to work for several months with Norman Maclaren at the National Film Board of Canada. This was an opportunity which Ormond particularly welcomed because he cherished the idea of establishing a comparable national unit in Wales. *I think we were all changed in the making of that film*, he wrote, and what he learned was eventually to appear in his poetry as well as in his films.

A few years after making BORROWED PASTURE Ormond relinquished what was becoming a rather onerous administrative post as head of a rapidly expanding film unit in order to become a film-maker in the features department of the BBC in Wales. He made more than eighty films during his career; the bread-and-butter output (Harry Soan investigating rivers, a film celebrating Llangollen, an arts magazine programme, filmed readings by Burton) was regularly supplemented by finer fare, invariably related to his deepest interests. His social conscience found expression in films ranging from SONG IN A STRANGE LAND (a study of eastern religions in Cardiff's dockland made in 1964) through THE COLLIERS' CRUSADE (his 1979 film about the part played by miners in the Spanish Civil War) to the late work, FAR FROM PARADISE, an environmental series directed by Brian Turvey for which he acted as consultant, as well as writing and narrating the commentary, while struggling with a debilitating illness. His interest in history from ancient to modern led to two series of THE LAND REMEMBERS (1972 and 1974), each consisting of five films in which Gwyn Williams (Trefenter) explored the Welsh past from earliest times to the present. Ormond had already covered one dramatic episode in recent Welsh history by visiting Patagonia in 1962 to make both a Welsh-language and an English-language film about Y Wladfa. THE DESERT AND THE DREAM conveniently illustrates a strength and a weakness of his film-making: his lack of Welsh and Spanish paradoxically licensed him to write a fine commentary keyed to the actual visual images that had been selected, but meant that his resulting portrait of the expatriate 'Welsh' community somewhat lacked historical depth and investigative insight. Ormond's films tended always to be intuitively attuned to their subject rather than analytical, although his stylish study of THE LIFE AND DEATH OF PICTURE POST (1977) is a partial exception and is a valuable historical document.

Yet, for all this steady output, invariably professional in standard and sometimes genuinely distinguished, there is a feeling among some of his colleagues and friends (though by no means shared by all) that from around the mid-sixties Ormond began to lose his cutting edge as a film-maker. Many possible reasons have been advanced in support of this claim: the difficulty of improving on BORROWED PASTURE; an altered working atmosphere as the BBC changed out of all recognition; the early, unexpected death in 1965 of Hywel Davies, the incomparable inspirer, mentor and enabler who for Ormond and countless others uniquely embodied the creative genius of the Welsh BBC; the retirement shortly thereafter of Aneirin Talfan Davies, Hywel's spiritual twin; the departure for HTV of Ormond's close friend, Aled Vaughan. To these were eventually to be added other possible factors – his turning back to poetry (which may have been both partial cause and partial effect of his relative dissatisfaction), his sense of being marginalized as younger talents developed, of being resented for the special privileges (of time and of respect) he supposedly enjoyed as a guru of the old guard. To some, his apparent loss of impetus seemed reflected in the difficulty he had in generating new ideas, in efficiently organizing his time and in getting to grips with a changing scene. But it has also been reasonably pointed out that his disaffection and disillusionment with the BBC should be carefully distinguished from his feelings about film itself – which remained for him an enticing creative medium. Moreover, the response to his work at recent events such as the conference on the visual arts held in Aberystwyth suggests that he continues to be regarded with high respect by members of another generation, and that his films are still acknowledged to have set a benchmark for those who follow.

Viewed against this background, Ormond's increasing preoccupation, after 1965, with arts documentaries assumes a problematical character. This can be seen as his choice of the soft option, the result of which was a miscarriage of his talent as an original, creative film-maker, as a poet in film, and as a maker of deeply humane, socially concerned documentaries. But it may also be seen in more positive ways – as a born egalitarian's attempt to mediate modern art to a mass, democratic audience (just as Ormond also did in his skilful radio features on Glyn Jones, Gwyn Thomas and Ceri Richards), and as work profoundly important to himself as an artist. Ranging as they do across poetry, music and painting, these films may be seen as involving an unconscious attempt to reintegrate and focus his powers and to redefine himself both as film-maker and as writer. This would help to explain the peculiar power of these documentaries, because whatever their visual limitations (they have been challengingly described as coffee-table films) and their lack of creative and intellectual ambition (they are wonderfully empathetic but somehow fail to anatomize their subjects), they remain utterly compelling in their power to realize that particular vision of art that all the artists represented share to some extent.

What is that vision? The list of the artists profiled by Ormond offers the clue: Dylan Thomas, Alun Lewis, Vernon Watkins, R. S. Thomas, Ceri Richards, Josef Herman, Daniel Jones, Graham Sutherland, Kyffin Williams – they are all, broadly speaking, modern Romantic artists who found expressionist means of rendering a world charged with energy and suffused with emotion. That Ormond was as conscious of this as he was uncomfortable with it is evident from the space which he devoted, when introducing a catalogue of Kyffin Williams's work, to the dubious argument that Williams is not a Romantic because *his art does nothing to engrandize what is already grand.* But what Ormond is really, and appropriately, saying is that Williams is not Romantic in the pejorative sense, that his work is thoroughly contemporary in idiom and should not be dismissed as old-fashioned.

Ormond's two films on Williams (the first in black and white, the second in colour) are oblique self-portraits as well as penetrating portraits. (Indeed portraiture was one art Ormond and Williams had in common, along with an enchanting gift for story-telling.) The painter's good-natured scorn for mainstream opinion, the stubborn integrity of his unfashionable style, his steady intention to produce his best work in middle age, his combination of a formalist interest in design with a 'puritanical' (his own word) insistence on mimetic fidelity, and his concept of the artist as artisan (he is heard wishing that modern artists could be as anonymous as medieval craftsmen) are all characteristics shared by Ormond. So, too, is Williams's belief in the (non-religious) spirituality of art, and his sensual passion both for the world of light and for his artistic medium – so recklessly does he apply paint that it costs him a fortune, he cheerfully explains! And an important if unspoken subject of both the films is the Romantic enigma of the artistic temperament. On the one hand Kyffin Williams is as ordinary as they come, happily rooted in Anglesey, a friendly chap among chaps; on the other hand he is afflicted with epilepsy, paints as he does because his pupils painfully fail to contract in sunlight, and is as solitary as he is sociable. The painful peculiarity of the artist is mentioned by Williams himself when, grateful though he is for the medication that controls his epilepsy, he reflects that had it been available in Van Gogh's time the Dutchman would have been an infinitely worse painter but an infinitely happier man.

This fascinated yet troubled sense of the otherness of the artist had haunted Ormond ever since he had first seen Ceri Richards in Ebenezer Chapel. It was no doubt an element in his friendship with colourful characters such as Dylan Thomas and John Tripp; and it surfaces very strongly in his film about that ultimate modern Romantic, Vernon Watkins, a film that opens with stunning shots of Three Cliffs Bay and of the lean poet walking in solitary splendour on the seashore. Here, as elsewhere in Ormond's work, one is reminded of the marvellously atmospheric rendering of artistic locales in the incomparable expressionist photographs of Bill Brandt, who had worked for PICTURE POST and had supplied some of the images for Ormond's NEWS CHRONICLE verses. Juxtaposed with these panoramas in UNDER A BRIGHT HEAVEN are constricted domestic shots of Watkins at home with his family, including a splendid interview with the forthright Gwen Watkins who ruefully observes that to be married to a poet is to find oneself in eternal fruitless competition with his true mistress, the Muse. This is a situation with which, one suspects, Glenys Ormond was herself resignedly familiar and about which Ormond himself had deeply ambiguous feelings. It is possible to see a tribute to his wife concealed in Ormond's affection-ate radio portrait of Ceri Richards's widow, Frances, a notable painter in her own right who, in addition, had provided her husband with strong practical and artistic support.

In all his films about artists, Ormond unfailingly places himself at the service of each artist's vision. This is both a sign of the generously excursive power of his imagination (evident in BORROWED PASTURE and in his poem-portraits) and an example of how film could provide him with the means of vicariously satisfying the imaginative needs of his own nature. So, for instance, his personal sense of *the miraculous poise of life between light and darkness* is worked out in Watkins's terms in UNDER A BRIGHT HEAVEN, while in treating Ceri Richards's paintings Ormond naturally homes in on the artist's genius for finding metaphors *for ebb and flow, for fixity and transience,* and on his insistence that art does not depict life directly but finds forms equivalent to it. Ormond loves to let artists speak for themselves, allowing Kyffin Williams to talk uninterruptedly for minutes on end and sanctioning the camera to dwell on a bare easel as Williams, oblivious to everything save the rapt train of his own thoughts, goes hunting for the picture he has in his mind. The printed transcipt of the remarks made to camera by R. S. Thomas in R. S. THOMAS: PRIEST AND POET offers invaluable insights into his poetics, even though the film in other ways illustrates the limitations of both Ormond's method and the medium. Failing to get on with a poet whose temperament and politics were so markedly different from his own, Ormond was unable – because of the obligations to a 'co-operating' subject which are always a hidden factor in the making of such films, and because of the instinctively empathetic cast of his own imagination – to produce a film illuminating Thomas's work by cutting *against* the grain of his convictions. For related reasons, Ormond was able to make little of the political dimensions of Thomas's work, which had been so particularly evident during the decade before the making of the film in 1972.

III

If his work in film contributed indirectly to Ormond's development as a writer, it also did so directly, since he dated his re-emergence as a poet to an epiphanic moment in Arezzo in 1963 when, making his documentary FROM A TOWN IN TUSCANY, he heard workmen whistling and singing high up in the campanile of the church. Some time later, or so he came to recall, the poem 'Cathedral Builders' came to him

in 50 minutes flat . . . It just seemed to come down my arm without my thought, and it broke the blockage that had kept me virtually silent for so many years. It was like nothing I had ever written before.

This liberation (which seems to have resulted in a finished poem some two years after the actual event in Arezzo) was also retroactive, in that it granted him creative access to past experience – Glenys Ormond has explained how memories from many years earlier of nervously climbing *sketchy ladders* to interview the Dean of Llandaff high up in the cathedral tower were incorporated into his Arezzo poem. And almost as important as the psychological (and stylistic) breakthrough was the availability to Ormond, virtually from the beginning of his re-emergence as a poet, of a ready and receptive poetry magazine where his work could be both tested and showcased. POETRY WALES, launched by Meic Stephens in the spring of 1965, was in one way the conscious successor to WALES and THE WELSH REVIEW of the early forties, in which some of Ormond's earliest poetry had appeared. Appropriately enough, 'Cathedral Builders' was (along with 'Design for a Tomb') the first piece he published in POETRY WALES (summer 1966), and over the next twenty years almost two dozen of his poems appeared there, among them many of the most celebrated. In Meic Stephens he also found someone who could share his passionate concern with not only the abstruser technicalities of poetry but also the finer points of typography. Ormond became noted for his erudite fascination with every aspect of book-production, lay-out and typography. It was of course another outlet for his graphic talents, but the fascination with print also dated back to his time at the PICTURE POST when the duties of the journalist included seeing the magazine through the press.

Our first commitment is to the craft, wrote Meic Stephens in his first POETRY WALES editorial (spring 1966); *Our second is to the country.* With the first Ormond was entirely in accord, but with the second he could have only qualified and guarded sympathy. While staunchly Welsh in his commitments according to his own lights, he had strong reservations about those particular forms of Welshness – a politico-cultural nationalism centred primarily on the Welsh language – which POETRY WALES came most to favour. Ormond's attitude towards Welsh is an important, complex and sensitive subject, upon which this essay can only touch. Key facts should be borne in mind: his father came from a family that had been monoglot English for generations; half his mother's family spoke Welsh, the other half (including herself) English; as a boy he attended a Welsh-language chapel; his wife Glenys is a Welsh-speaker; he himself had only a smattering of the language. This is a configuration of circumstances familiar to any south Walian; equally familiar is the spectrum of feelings deriving from it, usually resulting in a deep ambivalence of attitude which may find both creative and destructive expression. In certain ways, Welsh is the important Other for an English-language poet like John Ormond: his life is lived and his work done with continuous, yet usually unconscious, reference, to it. And working as he did in the BBC, the ongoing inter-language rivalries and resentments sadly endemic to that institution (relating to senior appointments, promotions, budgets, etc.) no doubt served only to exacerbate the situation.

Ormond had produced Welsh-language films and had many Welsh-speaking colleagues and friends (most of them, like Aneirin Talfan Davies, Gwyn Williams (Trefenter), Aled Vaughan and Glyn Jones, notably eirenic in outlook). However, the language-based nationalism which powered the revival of the sixties, and to which POETRY WALES was sympathetic, was anathema to him, except when encountered in the frankly maverick form so colourfully displayed by his friend and fellow poet, John Tripp, whose talents and manners he vainly tried to discipline. It was important therefore to his developing sense of himself as poet from the sixties onwards to have a network of friendships which helped offset powerful contemporary cultural trends to which he was hostile. Some of these friendships, for example his close, creative one with the Sussex-based poet, Ted Walker, related partly to his desire (very evident from his earliest days) to be judged not by parochial but by international standards of art. He had long craved and deeply appreciated international recognition, and having earned it in the form of awards for several of his films, he eventually repeated the feat as a poet: Oxford University Press published his DEFINITION OF A WATERFALL (1973); he received a Welsh Arts Council bursary, and several prizes; Penguin included him in its Modern Poets series, a Cholmondely award came his way; and a year before his death he was presented with the gold medal of Georgetown University in the USA. Other friendships, however, reflected his growing reorientation of himself with reference to anglophone, industrial south Wales. In a moving tribute delivered at his memorial service, Dai Smith (a noted historian of this culture and community) aptly identified him as being

of his tribe, of our tribe, a South Walian born into a South Wales that did, for a time, successfully demolish the freemasonry of group rule and parochial shibboleths which occasionally combine to stifle human creativity in countries such as ours.

Friendships with writers such as Gwyn Thomas, Alun Richards, Dai Smith, Glyn Jones, Patrick Hannan and Ron Berry belonged roughly in this category. Yet other friendships, however, placed him in the elective company of those who, to adopt Meic Stephens's distinction, believed that commitment to craft virtually ruled out commitment to country. Poets such as Dannie Abse and Leslie Norris – both based outside Wales – represented a form of political and cultural non-alignment which Ormond no doubt found deeply attractive during a period in Wales when *engagé* art (much of which must have seemed, to one of his temperament, little better than agitprop writing) was becoming the norm.

Leslie Norris, one of those against whose sensitive reactions Ormond most liked to test his poems, has also drawn attention to other suggestive features of their case. In his elegy for his friend, he recalled him as one who *moved out as I did, but returned,/ following his eyes and crossed the borders/ into his own country*. As one who returned in the late forties, Ormond is strikingly different from those exiles – such as Tony Conran, John Tripp, Sally Roberts Jones – whose return during the fifties and sixties was prologue to their commitment to the national, and in many cases nationalist, cause. But of course *into his own country* is a calculatedly ambiguous phrase, referring astutely to the sense in which Ormond's country (like that of Norris, so it is implied) is the unique, boundariless and therefore unbounded, country of his own imagination.

That is indeed an important part of the way in which Ormond as poet saw himself. But it is by no means the whole. In his great essay on attachment to place, Wallace Stevens characterizes artists as people whose very passion for a locality causes them to distance themselves from it in an attempt to comprehend it intellectually:

it may be said that they cease to be natives. They become outsiders. Yet it is certain that, at will, they become insiders again. In ceasing to be natives they have become insiders and outsiders at once.

This became, I believe, a valuable cast of Ormond's mind, which found expression in ways not only expected but unexpected: in his interest in convinced cultural migrants such as Dannie Abse, Kyffin Williams, Ceri Richards; in those love poems written across a distance to his wife; in the importance to him in later years of his periodic stays in Cortona, an Italian town one of whose attractions was paradoxically the unique vantage point it afforded him on his life in Wales. In a sense, his dedication to the concept of craft was itself the aesthetic counterpart of this mental trait, since it signalled his need to possess as well as to be possessed by his most intimate feelings. Be that as it may, Ormond's friendships seem, in some instances, to incorporate this aspect of his make-up, his need to cultivate a detached attachment.

Take, for instance, his admiration for the short stories of Glyn Jones and the fiction of Gwyn Thomas. In both cases he was particularly attracted to the mordancy of their knowing affection for, and affectionate knowledge of, their south Wales communities. That such insider knowledge combustively combined with outsider nous naturally found expression in fantasticating wit and bizarrerie of humour made it, of course, even more to the taste of an Ormond whose imagination was itself frequently that way inclined. Bitingly witty though he could, however, be in private conversation, and exhilarating though he famously was as raconteur, when it came to humorous representation of his community he allowed his imagination to compromise itself far too often, settling for insider complicitousness with the comfortable self-image of the society he was depicting. This could certainly result in enormously talented and attractive anecdotalism, such as his reminiscences of the exploits of the Dunvant village cricket team, featuring the captaincy of Ormond's uncle Alf, whose *spectacles were deep transfixed whirlpools of glass.* Alf's speciality was spinning wildly inventive explanations for his premature dismissal from the crease. From him *we learned the stammered truth of the unyielding falsity of things*:

An off-break would have skidded on a daisy malformed in one petal, so becoming an unplayable leg-break. A small towel, hung out to dry in a garden far beyond the boundary would have flapped and deflected the precise quantity of breeze required to transform a googlie into a lucky straight delivery. A mole would have hiccupped under a stump, removing a bail.

This is indeed rich, in several senses of the word, and comes from a rich vein of humour in Ormond's own make-up, as friends have affectionately recalled, and as is obvious from such asides (in letters from Italy to Glyn Jones) as [in Florence] *get in the wrong lane and it's as if Garibaldi had never invented unity.* When a rickety borrowed car broke down in a rainstorm on one memorable occasion, the family flagged down the first passing vehicle, *which was tiny and shaped like a lady-bird whose parents were still collecting family allowance.* When, however, this infectious, irresistible humour is brought to bear on south Wales life, it becomes much more resistible. Indeed, a glance at the Alf episode may help explain why Ormond, granted a bursary by the Arts Council in 1973 to write an autobiography, was never able to complete the project. It also helps me, at least, to understand my unease about several of the celebrated Dunvant poems which Ormond wrote during the late sixties. As I try to explain later, it seems to me that it is only when he adopts a bifocal approach, and is able to see the village simultaneously as insider and outsider, that he produces compelling poetry.

Ormond's reappearance as a poet in the mid-sixties

may be seen as part of the return of what Leslie Norris has called *the lost generation,* meaning the group of Welsh poets, born in the 1920s, who, in their youth and early maturity, had been eclipsed by the fame and hijacked by the style of Dylan Thomas. Along with Ormond, Abse and Norris himself were notable members of that generation, and so it was natural for a sense of solidarity to develop between them. Each had been slowly, separately and perhaps painfully evolving a mode of writing distinct from the Dylanesque poetics of their youth, and so, individualized and personally assured though their mature styles eventually became, they all tended to favour a combination of the colloquial speaking voice (as most perfectly instanced in the poetry of Edward Thomas) and the singing line (which Abse saw as a Welsh characteristic displayed to advantage in the poetry of Dylan Thomas but sadly abandoned by R. S. Thomas).

Although Ormond came later to emphasize the break between his earlier and later poetic self, when he published his first collection REQUIEM AND CELEBRATION in 1969 he decided to print the poems *only very roughly* [in] *the order in which they were written.* This may have been not only because of his concern to suggest a *development and unity* but also because many of the early poems had been substantially revised for publication. Of the thirty-six poems in this volume, thirteen were not thereafter to reappear in any subsequent selection, nine were next to be gathered only in his final SELECTED POEMS, and only seven were to recur in all three of his later selections. But although many of his major poems had not yet been completed in 1969, REQUIEM AND CELEBRATION signalled the emergence of a clearly significant voice, which was welcomed by Glyn Jones (on the book's dustjacket) as the product of a long struggle, begun as far back as 1944, to establish *a vital connection . . . between lived experience and its expression in the poetry.* Dannie Abse was also impressed and subsequently featured Ormond's poetry in CORGI MODERN POETS IN FOCUS: 5 in 1973.

In the same year the prestigious Oxford University Press published Ormond's new selection, DEFINITION OF A WATERFALL, with the announced intention of bringing *his poems to the notice of a much wider audience* than that in his native Wales. The backcover blurb characterized him as a rooted south Walian *with a finely-gauged control over language and with a subtle affection that informs all his work.* Hastening to add that his poems were as universal in appeal as they were local in origin, the blurb spoke of Ormond's *need to come to terms with the uneasy flux which the human consciousness bears. The poetry is the definition of this state: the definition is the answer to its threat.* There was also a mention of *a painter's eye for detail and a musician's ear for rhythm and sound.* Only ten of the twenty-eight poems in this collection had already appeared in REQUIEM AND CELEBRATION. Among the new additions were 'Certain Questions for Monsieur Renoir', 'Salmon', and 'The Piano Tuner'.

That *painter's eye* was one which Ormond himself felt he was continuing to train through his work in film – the professional work upon which, of course, he continued to be employed until his retirement from the BBC in 1984. And not only was his poetry written in parallel with this, there were also many important points of convergence in his two careers.

For instance, in 1968 while working on his film biography of Alun Lewis (for whom he had himself published an elegy in 1945) he was encouraged to show his poems to one of Lewis's shrewdest inter- preters, the influential London critic Ian Hamilton. Hamilton's positive reaction, more or less coinciding with Meic Stephens's advice to clear out his mental attic so as to make room for new material, helped Ormond to muster up the courage to publish REQUIEM AND CELEBRATION. A film could also spawn a poem, as when a short documentary about Wales's great salmon-fishing rivers, televised in 1965, started Ormond working on 'Salmon'. Searching for a location where wheat could be seen lapping at a great ancient cromlech – an image needed for A BRONZE MASK, his fine elegiac tribute to Dylan Thomas (1968) – Ormond found the central symbol of his superb poem, 'Ancient Monuments'.

As is true of most poets, Ormond came by his poems in many, unpredictable ways and at unexpected times – or perhaps it was they that came upon him: he was fond of repeating Vernon Watkins's remark that the Muse did not keep sensible hours. Some were produced in a short, set time, in response to a friendly competitive challenge from Leslie Norris or Ted Walker – 'Where Home Was' originated as an exercise about bridges, and 'Summer Mist' as a poem about friendship. He agonized over others for an eternity, laboriously constructed, deconstructed, and reconstructed, revised interminably, and only grudgingly released them for publication. The starting-point might be a phrase (the *starched eyes* of a piano-tuner), a rhythm, a feeling, or a visual experience: 'Lazarus' was triggered by the unnerving syndrome from which his friend Wynne Williams suffered, a medical condition that caused him to be briefly paralysed upon awaking from sleep, totally immobilized and unable to move a single muscle. Verbal doodling could sometimes lead to something serious – evidence, as Ormond put it, that *presumably the poem was there all the time*. Or starting in one way, a poem would end in another, as when an elegy for Marilyn Monroe turned into 'Design for a Tomb', after Ormond had visited Juliet's reputed tomb in Verona. His intense concern that the right note be struck, and the appropriate form chosen, right from the very start did not mean that he would never revise his original decision: 'The Key' began as a tight formal structure, but was eventually relaxed to allow closer approximation to *ordinary speech rhythms and indeed ordinary vocabulary*.

In general, poems either came quite quickly to Ormond, or seemed to play coy for an eternity. Poems could be hurriedly written for special occasions, most notably when Ormond had forgotten to buy Glenys an anniversary present. 'In September' was one such, finished at a single, frantic, late-night sitting. When Glyn Jones celebrated his seventieth birthday in 1975, Ormond lovingly honoured the occasion by presenting him with a sequence of poems roughly, but resourcefully, modelled on the syllabics and metrics of the Welsh *englyn* form:

> *Merthyr man, natty dresser – his tweed hats*
> *Have no more fine possessor.*
> *They fit like cup to saucer.*
> *Dandy, too, in language, sir.*

In a like spirit, Ormond would send personalized birthday and Christmas cards to friends, each consisting of a poem beautifully illustrated by hand. A burning sun surrounded by curling shapes of falling leaves that resembled licking flames was the motif illustrating 'A Lost Word'; a sketch of a grandfather clock accompanied 'Right Time'; 'Design for a Quilt' was imaged by the ornately branching trunk of an embroidered tree, adorned with stylized birds. To see the poems reproduced in this way is to appreciate anew that for Ormond, as for certain other poets with spectacular graphic gifts, from Blake to Lear to Brenda Chamberlain, there was an intimate, symbiotic relationship between visual image and printed word. No wonder he felt particularly close to a writer such as Glyn Jones, who was himself an artist manqué, and to a strong image-maker, like their mutual friend, the painter John Elwyn.

The exuberance of an entertaining poem such as 'The Birth of Venus at Aberystwyth' is a reminder that, though he was never comfortable with the performance culture of the sixties as typified by the lightly politicized poems-and-pints sessions popular during this period, Ormond was a stylish participant in poetry readings, whether formal or informal in character. Ron Berry has recalled that 'Salmon' was

first read . . . in a Cardiff pub (Anglo-Welsh gathering, February 1970 or thereabouts) and also 'Cathedral Builders', first publicly launched a couple/few years previously in a Port Talbot pub (night of the eisteddfod).

But Ormond was a reluctant public performer of his own work: his preferred version of poems and pints took the form of attendance at the Conway and the Romilly, where – wide-ranging in his interests, intellectually curious, and a vividly entertaining and illuminating talker – he could socialize informally or scribble quietly in a corner, as often as not doodling sketches of other customers, rather than taking dictation from the Muse as conveniently rumoured. But if Ormond clearly relished and thrived on the creative stimulus of this camaraderie, he equally clearly needed to isolate, and insulate, himself periodically, in order to give his writing time to consolidate into substantial, considered form. He would work impulsively, and compulsively, deep into the night in his room at home in Conway Road, invariably showing the drafts next morning to his wife, Glenys, whose criticism he particularly appreciated. And, from the early eighties onwards, he greatly cherished both his connections, through his friend Michael Collins, with Fordham University (USA), which boasted a summer campus near Florence, and his annual retreats to the beautiful Tuscan town of Cortona, in Arezzo province, which he came to regard as his second home. There, *long-felt ideas and long-heard music seem . . . to cohere*, he gratefully recorded: it was one of *those places that unlock words in me*.

Able to speak little Italian, Ormond originally found that his stays in Cortona curbed his usually incorrigible impulse to socialize and defamiliarized English for him so that he was resensitized to its extraordinary resources. Freed from his established social identity, he was able to reactivate neglected aspects of himself – most importantly, he found the confidence, in the context of a different culture where art had a natural place and value, to identify himself firmly as a poet. When asked what he did, he would reply *Sono poeta*, relishing as he did so the allusion to LA BOHÈME. His life at Cortona was relaxed, yet disciplined by a steady routine which suited one who had produced so much of his best work to deadlines. And while the food and wine brought out the cosmopolitan *bon viveur* in him, the beauty of the old town fed the connoisseur of fine art who had originally dreamt of becoming a painter or architect. He loved the intricate geometry of roofs and walls, and the flitting, arcing, swooping flight of the swifts:

> *The swifts are invisibly mending the sky*
> *Where last night's wind tore it to pieces,*
> *Stitching, delirious with light labour,*
> *High on it, with dizzy double-darning*
> *Done in twos. Such work's a tall order.*

His identification with these resourceful, practised and practical artists is evident, not least when he fondly pretends to chide their anarchic tendencies, the untidiness of these *natural/ Non-joiners* who are *fellow-travellers*. Indeed the playful distinction which he makes in this poem between his impulse to unionize the swifts and his contrary impulse simply to enjoy and sing their wayward creative freedom, is a light-hearted reminder of splits that have already been noted as key to his character: the split between freedom and discipline, socio-political commitment and non-alignment, participation in the collective and the originality that comes only with unfettered individualism. Earlier versions of the poem show him toying with cognate images he later discarded: *The swifts are putting their summer/ Decorations up above the walls of the square/ Like Christmas streamers.* He also played, for a while, with an elaborated image of the sky:

Sky being the loftiest
Of ladies to be redressed,
Presenting herself, it seems,
Patchy at the best of times;
Except when blue, she's serene
And serenaded by sun,
Coquetting with small white clouds
Like a high queen forgetting
Her hautère, forgiving
Meaningless lèse-majesté.

Such drafts – and there are literally hundreds among his unsorted papers – display his love of extended conceits, his instinctive recourse to word-play ('serene . . . serenaded') and pun ('redressed'), and his sometimes conflicting impulses to elaborate and to compress.

Ormond certainly was a tireless reviser and double-darner of his work, almost obsessively reluctant to abandon his work to publication. As his papers show, he was also fascinated by the kaleidoscopic effects that could be produced by presenting his poems in a variety of sequences and combinations. In fact, DEFINITION OF A WATERFALL (1973) was the last 'new' collection which he published, since in the PENGUIN MODERN POETS series his work appeared alongside that of John Tripp and Emyr Humphreys, while his SELECTED POEMS collected together the best work from every phase of his career. But his papers show that he was experimenting with various titles (and contents lists) for projected volumes. 'Words of a Common World' was one such, as was 'Bright Yellow Umbrella', a title keyed to an attractive sketch for a poem that sadly exists only in draft:

In the shop window, its audacity;
Yellow handle, yellow ferrule.

> *And, tested for its taut dispute*
> *The eccentricity*
> *Of its dispute with the sun;*
> *Because despite itself it's about rain*
> *. . . one of those sunflowers*
> *That sad man painted, who*
> *Always cheered me up, in bright*
> *Dispute with death.*

Death had for him always been an important motive for poetry. He had repeatedly attempted to elegize the two old Polish farmers of BORROWED PASTURE: *What courtesies do you show each/ other now as you lie in the same/ grave?* he wondered, recalling that to the end they had continued to address each other, with an undiminished formality that granted no concession to the long years of familiarity, as *Pan.* Still unfinished at Ormond's own death was the elegy for Dylan Thomas – sharing with the film the working title 'A/The Bronze Mask' – upon which he had been engaged for so long, and of which Dannie Abse remains a very particular admirer.

As his friends began to pass away, Ormond's impulse to elegize understandably grew stronger. He even conceived the idea of a series of 'Letters to the Dead': among the recipients would have been B. S. Johnson (memorialized in 'Notes to a Suicide'), Ceri Richards and Graham Sutherland (commemorated respectively in 'Salmon' and 'Landscape in Dyfed'), his father, his mother, his Auntie Mary, Louis MacNeice, Vernon Watkins, Dylan Thomas, Gwyn Thomas, and 'The dead in general'. The elegy for Gwyn Thomas, dated 1984, includes several fine unfinished passages:

> *Those missing faces that the night retrieves,*
> *Vivid, alive and vanishing; waking*

Into the dark, we are no longer
Part of what they are; they and we
Inhabit different darknesses.

In lines that reveal requiem to involve celebration, Thomas is exultantly recalled as an *Assassin of pomposity, this killer only by wounds/ Of deep unhealing laughter, this javeline-thrower/ Of verbs*. Ormond's celebrated kindness to his friends, whether living or departed, was by no means confined to words. He was instrumental in securing a Civil List Pension for several, including his old friend, Ron Berry, and he worked hard to disentangle Gwyn Thomas's affairs after his death. By way of tribute to that comic genius, he staged LAUGHTER BEFORE NIGHTFALL (OR, THE MAN WHO RUBBED THE RAINBOW), a compilation culled from the 'wit and work' of Gwyn Thomas. Sharing Thomas's devotion to laughter, Ormond also shared his sense of the ambivalence of comedy's reading of life: *Humour*, Thomas is appreciatively quoted as saying, *is a nervous condition. Listen to laughter. It has a strange, sinister sound; the yelping of an uneasy pack*. LAUGHTER BEFORE NIGHTFALL, as performed by Ray Smith and Emrys James, aimed to capture the dark duplicitousness of Thomas's comic imagination.

Ormond also paid homage to the talents of his friends in radio programmes which he scripted, in essays and reviews, in memorial addresses (such as the one for Graham Sutherland, delivered at Westminster Cathedral) and in brilliant essays in catalogues of exhibitions by Kyffin Williams and Ceri Richards. In the process he not infrequently revealed something of importance about himself, as when he concluded a review of Gwyn Thomas's work by quoting lines from SAP, recording a determination to *project some sound of love from the core of what I was and am. The world will bend its head to hear. And the world won't give a damn!* The distinctive texture of his own poems is obliquely suggested by his comments on Glyn Jones's short fiction:

The stories, still reading well aloud, are as much fabricated as told. In that sense the verbal concentration has something in common with a complex embroidery where the detail, in its brilliance, demands a slower progress of the eye.

His long, perceptive essay about Dannie Abse's poetry is peppered with observations that incidentally pinpoint affinities between Abse's imagination and his own. Abse, characterized sympathetically as a 'vulnerable' man, is praised for 'the consistency of his timbre', for the quality of his poetic portraiture and for the way, ever since recovering from the influence of Dylan Thomas, he had avoided the least hint of pretentiousness. Noting Abse's fondness for remarking that *a vision dies from being too long stared at,* Ormond is appreciative of his poetry's subtle acknowledgement that *mysteries are insoluble, cannot be ignored, and are, in fact, needed.* Ormond argues that *The need for something in the vacuum of belief, 'the thirst that from the soul doth rise', is unassuagable . . . We are always on the haunted brink of what might be revealed.* His conclusion could double as a kind of personal credo: *Perhaps it is not possible to be an artist without religious inclination, no matter how seemingly self-practising.*

A book of poems is like an exhibition of paintings, Ormond characteristically remarked to Richard Poole: *you put in things which hang together and bounce off one another even if they are separated in time, in years and after many years.* It is a revealing comment that helps explain not only his deliberate avoidance of exact chronology in REQUIEM AND CELEBRATION but also the structure, for instance, of his film about Dylan Thomas, A BRONZE MASK, in which the bust of the poet, displayed at the National Museum of Wales, is juxtaposed with other paintings and pieces of sculpture to be seen there, thus providing a sequence of contrasting images around which Ormond is able to construct a thematic collage of poetry. This spatial imagination, evident also in his memorable films about painters, is what made Ormond such a stickler about every aspect of the lay-out, from arrangement of page to arrangement of contents, of his SELECTED POEMS. Published by Seren in 1987, this is likely to remain the definitive collection of Ormond's poetry. It gathers together work spanning some forty years, omitting little of genuine significance, and groups the poetry into five sections that are both roughly chronological and broadly thematic. Distinctions that Ormond was himself fond of making – between his poetry of kinship and his aesthetic poetry, his Welsh poems and his cosmopolitan poems, his love poetry and his elegies, his relatively plain writing and his relatively intricate writing – are reflected in these groupings. And the fifth and last section consists of poems he himself felt to be unclassifiable: he explained to Poole, for instance, that 'Soliloquies of a Secret Policeman' was the nearest he had ever come to automatic writing, since this, the most overtly political of his poems, had virtually forced itself upon his bewildered attention.

SELECTED POEMS was the last volume of his poetry to

be published during Ormond's lifetime. It was sadly left to his wife, Glenys, and his daughter, Rian, to oversee the final stages of the publication of CATHEDRAL BUILDERS, the beautiful limited edition with accompanying sketches by Ormond's own hand, brought out by the distinguished Gregynog Press in 1991. Very mindful of the Press's long-standing and unrivalled reputation for special editions of the very highest quality, Ormond had been delighted to be invited not only to publish with them but also to advise on the design of the book. His dissatisfaction with the illustrations that were originally suggested led to an agreement that the text be adorned with drawings he would himself make specially for the edition. Sadly this proved impossible, owing to his rapidly deteriorating health. Instead, after his death his wife and daughter drew upon the sketches he had made years before, in a collection of poems which he had presented to Glenys, inspired by a similar gift Ceri Richards had fashioned for his wife, Frances.

'Blue Bath Gown', the lovely late poem included in CATHEDRAL BUILDERS, is evidence that Ormond's talent as a poet was not in decline towards the end, as that of his friend, Dylan Thomas, had been rumoured to be by 1953. Indeed, in addition to a mass of unfinished work – some of which was promising poetry on which Ormond had been intermittently working for many years – the papers that survive include sketches for ambitious projects, such as 'the Italian suite', a collection of poems relating to the artistic treasures of several great Italian cities. The Ravenna mosaics particularly fascinated him – a book on that subject was among those returned by Glenys Ormond to the local library shortly after his death – not least perhaps because, as Richard Poole has astutely noted, his own poetry resembles what Ormond himself, wryly conscious of coining an oxymoron, called *an organic mosaic.*

Ormond died, at the age of sixty-seven, on 4 May 1990. Although he had not been seriously unwell, he had for some time suffered from an underlying heart condition, probably caused by the two severe bouts of rheumatic fever from which he had suffered as a child. Unfortunately, the condition had gone undetected until he was in his sixties. A few years before his death he had also contracted a debilitating disease which at first baffled medical opinion, but was eventually diagnosed and successfully treated thanks to an unlikely, yet wholly characteristic, train of events. Periodically ill with malaria-like bouts of fever, he nevertheless generously placed his home in Cardiff at the disposal of friends of his friend, Seamus Heaney, who were on a visit to Wales from the United States. As it happened, the husband of one of these visitors was a distinguished specialist in tropical diseases. When informed of Ormond's symptoms, he was able to diagnose Lyme Disease, an illness then little known, which Ormond had contracted during his long stay near Florence in the winter of 1983–4.

The warmth of the tributes paid to Ormond after his death was affectingly unforced. Although he could sometimes seem grand seigneurial in manner towards those for whom he felt little respect or liking, to his friends he was impulsively generous, unstintingly companionable, inexhaustibly informative and sometimes wickedly entertaining. His mannerisms further endeared him to them, and some of these were slyly caught, in a spirit of appropriately comic tribute, by Dai Smith. *He snaps his eyes open and shut, open and wrinkled again,* he wrote in 1980,

his neck thrusting out his head in emphasis, like a tortoise approaching the truth of a lettuce leaf, then his mouth clamps abruptly on his words. He swivels his head, dissatisfied, amused with himself, wondering if you'd rather hear a well-turned anecdote.

Ormond was himself rather ruefully amused by Smith's description, just as he playfully resented the *bola* with which he had been provided in his old friend John Elwyn's striking portrait of him. And Ormond's distinctively emphatic and unpredictably blurting manner of speaking – still to be heard on the soundtracks of his films as well as on the record he made of his own poetry – has been well characterized in Smith's description of *his breathing staccato, that parenthetically-inflected voice with its unexpected trip-wire stopping.* Ron Berry, seeing the inner man embodied in such mannerisms, wrote feelingfully of

the good man John, his hard tempered, earned innocence. He rarely had to erupt, tantrum, dudgeon, but he could with splendid impunity. More often he spurted delight or slowed down to insight, the prolonged 'a-a-and' while searching for a proper, apocryphal or dissident verdict. Joy convulsed him, creased his eyes. Matching whatever ideas, his fine androgynous hands were mesmeric whether loading a kebab skewer or discreetly scrunching, passing a note to pay for the next round.

Most moving of all, in its blending of dignity, honesty and gaiety of grateful affection, was his wife Glenys's short portrait of one who had been her best friend.

Returning home to Conway Road from hospital, on the evening of John Ormond's passing, the subdued family noticed that builders, working on a neighbour's house, had left their *sketchy ladders* pointing skywards, if not heavenwards. It seemed a fitting elegy; an appropriately visual quotation.

IV

Although the romantic is referred to, most often, in a pejorative sense, this sense attaches, or should attach, not to the romantic in general but to some phase of the romantic that has become stale. Just as there is always a romantic that is potent, so there is always a romantic that is impotent.

Not only do Wallace Stevens's words illuminate the means by which he deliberately remade himself into one of the great modern masters (immensely admired by John Ormond as an inspiringly instructive case), they also highlight the self-refashioning careers of many leading mid-twentieth-century writers and artists, including Philip Larkin (an early admirer of Vernon Watkins), Robert Lowell and John Berryman (who began as American Apocalyptic poets), and Graham Sutherland (who was devoted early to William Blake and Samuel Palmer). In significantly different ways, the mature work of each of these is the successful outcome of a personal stylistic struggle to transform the *romantic that is impotent* into *the romantic that is potent*. John Ormond's long period of virtual elective muteness as a poet may itself have been the outward sign of a similar inner struggle, one which was partly obscured by and partly enacted through his successful career as a film-maker during that time.

If one is looking for the possible script of that particular self-recreative drama, one could do worse than turn to Dannie Abse's prescient editorial note in

POETRY AND POVERTY 1952 (No.14). After noting the origins of the New Romanticism in a reaction both to the Audenesque thirties poetry of social commitment and to the *Vera Lynn clamour* of wartime solidarity, Abse concedes that much of the visceral poetry produced in the grand Apocalyptical manner was indeed as described by the *Poetry Headmaster of the thirties*, Geoffrey Grigson: *altogether self-indulgent and liquescent. An Ink Cap mushroom grows up white and firm and then flops down into a mess of ink – which is our new romance.* However, Abse sensibly continues, the best of the work was appreciably better than that and should not be superciliously dismissed in favour of the sedate new suburban classicism favoured by the Movement poets. *It is not, then, in this over-compensated reaction to Neo-Romanticism that the poetry of the fifties has hope of importance or readability,* Abse argues, *but rather, I believe, in the modification and development of the romantic vision of the poets of the last decade.* So Abse pleads for a second phase of Neo-Romanticism:

Certainly it is not enough to have a fury of images, or a devotion to musical patterns or eccentric typography. A disciplined romantic texture must be insisted upon. Romanticism must be tempered with an organic concept in its substance so that the concept at least on one level (preferably on more) may be fairly and honestly communicable. It is important though to understand that a poetic intelligence should correlate the wedding of aural and visual elements, not a prose one.

In many respects this anticipates Ormond's poetics from the mid-sixties onwards, and so reminds us that his mature poetry is in some ways as much a development as a repudiation of his early manner of writing (in its love of exuberance, its high verbal colour, its persistent musicality, its strong emotional charge), even though he himself understandably tended to emphasize the latter aspect.

In what remains the best profile of John Ormond and his work, Richard Poole quotes him as agreeing that the omission from SELECTED POEMS of almost all his early, symbolist pieces *amounted to a conscious rejection of his early style.* And yet the full picture is considerably more complicated, involving the interweaving of difference and continuity. As Jeremy Hooker has noted, Ormond remained a symbolist poet throughout his life, with the crucial difference that whereas his earlier symbolist poems were poeticized and derivative his later *poems work symbolically through credible realistic narratives and sensuously particularised descriptions. If symbolism is a universal language,* Hooker adds, *in poetry it is spoken only by those who have made it their own through personal experience.* And, as he further remarks:

Ormond's unique achievement is to combine the strengths of two important poetic movements: the symbolism of the Forties and Fifties, and the clarity and conversational 'naturalness' associated mainly with R. S. Thomas – though Ormond is more formal than Thomas.

But then, that 'clarity' was potentially there in his writing from the outset, coexisting at source with the symbolist impulse. Ormond's very first published poem, 'Collier' (1942), strikingly anticipated both in subject-matter and in directness of style the Dunvant poems of the later sixties; the latter are themselves, of course, prefaced by 'My Dusty Kinsfolk', which may have predated them by about fifteen years. In turn, that poem reminds us that as a *writer* Ormond had learnt, from earliest PICTURE POST days, to be stylistically flexible; this was a skill which he put to good use when he wrote the verses for the NEWS CHRONICLE, and of which he took most splendid poetic advantage when so memorably scripting A SORT OF WELCOME TO SPRING, a script which may be seen as an important bridging passage in his work. But before such a skill could become available to him as a resource for poetry, it seems, he had to modify his high Romantic sense of what poets were, what they did and in particular how they 'spoke'. As Richard Poole has perceptively pointed out, Ormond's *achieved maturity has very much to do with his realization of a natural speaking voice.*

It is perhaps no accident that his celebrated 'comeback' poem, 'Cathedral Builders', is, at least in part, an exercise in that important mode of inverted Romanticism, the anti-heroic (cf. Philip Larkin). *I bloody did that,* declare the stonemasons, as they cock up a squint eye at Romantically soaring arches and clerestories. But of course their defiantly down-to-earth idiom (a 'voice' representing a whole mode of experience and style of expression which is missing from Ormond's earlier poetry) only adds strength to what, climbing *on sketchy ladders* they have so undeniably achieved: *Inhabited sky with hammers, defied gravity,/ Deified stone, took up God's house to meet Him.* Romantic (if not Promethean?) heroism, most certainly, yes – but also again balanced (and ballasted) by more than a touch of the anti-heroic, this time in the form of ironizing ambiguities of meaning, derived directly from the pathos of Ormond's own agnosticism. Could it be that in so gloriously defying gravity all they have done is deify stone, in the sense of vainly attributing divinity to the brute matter of an untransfigurable world?

In his mature poetry, then, Ormond is constantly tempering his Romanticism with a scepticism which toughens it without destroying it. Humour becomes one exuberant, if not altogether successful, means of doing this. 'The Birth of Venus at Aberystwyth' is a skit bringing Botticelli to grief, as it were, on the rocks of darkest provincial Wales. Obviously a satire on killjoy, anti-aesthetic and anti-sensuous Nonconformity, it is also, however, a pseudo-Ovidean poem in which, a little like Wallace Stevens in such poems as 'The Comedian as the Letter C' or William Carlos Williams in his reading of Brueghel's fall of Icarus, Ormond passingly mocks his own yearnings for legendary beauty. His modern Venus nearly drowns, hobbling ashore *grazing her great toe*. But she makes it, so that *Her different world was added to the world*. Ormond's humour tends ultimately to be over-protective of the romantic values which it mocks. It consequently lacks the unsettling (because un-settled) power of his best wit, but can produce its own modest surprises. 'Lament for a Leg' is not only a lively comic poem; it is also a kind of conversation with Dafydd ap Gwilym in the form of an in-joke based on a deliberate pastiche of the great Welsh poet's manner of writing. It is, in fact, a poem much more in keeping with the boisterous, farcical, anarchic spirit of some of Dafydd's own work than is the piously sanitized Victorian image of him as *The pure poet who, whole, lies near and far/ From me, still pining for Morfudd's heart*.

'Lament for a Leg' can also be read as a playful variation on that staple Welsh form, the exile's romantic song of *hiraeth* – after all, the amputee bequeathes to Dafydd his *unexiled part*, the leg which he has left behind in Strata Florida! But some exiles find a permanent home on the other, tough, side of longing. In 1965 the Patagonian Welsh marked the centenary of their first arrival in Argentina, and the occasion was commemorated by Ormond (who had filmed in Y Wladfa a few years earlier) in 'Instructions to Settlers'. The poem is in fact deliberately *unsettling*, as it moves unpredictably in and out of perfect rhyme, mixing it with haphazard and approximate consonances of sound and syllable. The real sense of dependable orientation and of organizing energy is provided not by the rhymes that end lines but by the verbs that begin them: 'Dig deep', 'Cut through', 'Strike', 'Search', 'Work', 'Ease'. These are the verbal and physical imperatives by which the people make a life, and make a living, under harshly hostile conditions, struggling, as they do so, to survive in a *mistaken Canaan*. The parallels between this actual physical landscape and the inner, psychic landscape of Ormond himself, the one-time believer, are clear enough. And it is as if the power of a disregarded part of speech – the plain verb – had been made manifest under these conditions to a poet whose early romantic inclination had been to smother it with adjectives and adverbs.

Work stone and white to green./ Ease your tormented ghost, is Ormond's tough final benediction on the settlers' life, and as so often in his poetry sound becomes the portent and lubricant of sense: 'ease' seems to proceed naturally out of 'green', just as the cultivated fertility of the Chubut valley provides the settlers with sustenance. 'Green', as synonym for the positive aspect of the cycle of life, is a key term in Ormond's poetic lexicon, more or less consciously linking his secularized language and vision to those of Dylan Thomas (*The force that through the green fuse drives the flower*) and Wallace Stevens (whose post-Christian persona in 'Sunday Morning' famously protests there is no *cloudy palm/ Remote on heaven's hill, that has endured/ As April's green endures*). But in the sense in which it is used in 'The Gift' (the poem used as epigraph for SELECTED POEMS) the word strongly recalls Wittgenstein's language philosophy. Do not ask *From where, from whom?*, we are advised as we confront the cosmos: *Enough that it was given, green, as of right, when,/ Equally possible, nothing might ever have been.* Green is here the colour of the given, unalterable, nature of things; it represents the wonderful arbitrariness and arbitrary wonder of existence, which is possessed of a purely contingent internal coherence, and admits of no Romantic belief in either immanence or transcendence. And the questions we are warned not to ask about it are not so much questions for which we can find no answers as questions which, in Wittgenstein's terms, make no real sense because they lie beyond the limits that give meaning to language.

John Ormond's initially Wittgensteinian interest in the philosophy of language seems eventually to have extended to the structural linguistics of thinkers like Saussure. 'Illuminations of the Letter O' is a modern secular age's commentary on the exquisitely illuminated sacred manuscripts of a departed age of belief. Modern man is depicted as literally trapped in a letter, revealed to be a dependent creature of language, totally isolated from the *ding an sich* of the universe. In turn a letter is demonstrated to be a letter only by virtue of its relationships with other letters (the 'text') within the artifical structure of signs and sounds that constitute a 'language'. Otherwise the 'letter O', for instance, is literally nothing (or alternatively a zero), and of course without the letter O there would be no 'Ormond' . . . Human identity is then the 'subject' of language, and human beings are more the products than the producers of language, just as the figure trapped within the outline of the letter O, and so ambiguously figured that he could be mistaken for either shepherd or hunter, cannot walk at large, or at will, throughout the adjoining text. Nevertheless, man's state is depicted, in the second part of the poem, as cause for more than mourning, because if in one sense the mortal coil of that 'O' represents 'nothing', in another it represents 'wonder'; the wonder that accrues from participation in the circular dance of all existence, and from knowing, as Stevens put it, *the heavenly fellowship/ Of men that perish and of summer morn.*

Yet even as they repeatedly reaffirm this unillusioned vision of life, several of Ormond's poems tend almost imperceptibly towards the condition of elegy for a lost authenticating language of faith; a lingering sense, as he puts it in 'A Lost Word', of *characters imprinted/ On the other side of the page, in parallel* that *press through/ On what we are trying to say, and would disclose/ News or perhaps solace.* But such a fiction of solace is ultimately available only for children, as Ormond demonstrates, in a way that is both touching and desolating, in 'There There, Then', which can be read as his reworking of Hopkins's famous poem 'Spring and Fall'. 'There there, then', is the magically comforting formula routinely murmured by an adult to a child literally holding its breath after its first shocked exposure to the world's hurt. However, the familiar phrase takes on a sombre, hollow ring as the 'there' and the 'then' are revealed as locating the child inexorably in the 'here' and the 'now' of our mortal condition. In this poem language abandons its initial pretence of innocence and admits its knowledge of the dark facts of the human case:

> But why, child, why the fall?
> Ah, it's useless to say
> That that's a grave, bottomless notion
> And all to do, in the end,
> With gravity.

No longer can a resort to the doctrine of 'the Fall' explain a 'fall'. It is simply the way things are, the result of a life literally and metaphorically subject to the law of gravity, and of the grave that will be the final downfall of us all.

The poet must not adapt his experience to that of the philosopher warned Stevens, and Ormond certainly never did. But tutored as he had been by Rush Rhees, he did retain an interest in the philosophy of language that came to influence, albeit inconsistently and unsystematically, the way he used language in his poetry. The poem 'Saying' makes us out to be *Prisoners within those words/ We happen to know, captives behind/ Bars of arbitrary sound*. Grammar, syntax and vocabulary are all demonstrated to be the mere functions of mere phonemes. That way, of course, lies the post-modernist and post-structuralist emphasis on the prison house of language (the very image used by Ormond in 'Saying'). Read in such a light, several of his poems, conspicuously full as they are of sound patterns, become self-consuming artefacts, works which actively foreground the fact that all their elegances of meaning are instantaneously disassembling themselves into babble. But Ormond himself usually chose to stop short of the severe prison house of post-modernism, preferring instead the half-way house of Wallace Stevens's provocatively prevaricating post-Romantic way of putting things. *The final belief,* the American famously wrote, *is to believe in a fiction, which you know to be a fiction, there being nothing else.* And elsewhere he recorded his delight, as artist, in the freedom of such fictiveness, experienced as *The joy of meaning in design/ Wrenched out of chaos.*

Like Stevens, Ormond's obsession with design was, as he admitted, rooted in *the darker side of my life, an indication of my need for a sense of order. And this is clearly denied one who has lost the reassurances of a formal faith.* And again like Stevens, his sense of the fictiveness of art found periodic expression in his poetry through such devices and strategies of self-consciousness as archness of tone, equivocations of wit, mannered vocabulary and a bravura display of style that came naturally to one temperamentally attracted to hyperbole and conceit. This exhilaratingly extravagant mode of writing (well characterized as 'rococo' by Richard Poole) is displayed to best advantage in 'Certain Questions for Monsieur Renoir', which is fitting since after all it is a composition about a composition, a poem about a painting. The painting is Renoir's 'La Parisienne', and Ormond's response to it, brilliantly rendered as an inexhaustible cascade of tributary improvisations, reveals much about the fountainhead of art and the ambiguous terms of its gifts to life.

The vivid impression of a human being in Renoir's painting is shown to be essentially a by-product of the painter's primary compositional interest in the sensuality of colour. The painting is a tone-poem in pigment, so that the only answerable style for writing about it is a tone-poem in words, as is suggested in the poem's original title 'Blue Major'. The impulse to art, then, is the artist's passion for his medium (whether it be paint, or sound, or words), and it is paradoxically by prioritizing the exploration of that medium that an artist enriches his, and our, appreciation of life. An increase in our vocabulary, argued Stevens, means an increase in our feeling for reality. Ormond's excited response to the astonishing 'vocabulary' of a 'single' colour in Renoir's painting is to proliferate terms that distinguish innumerable shades and qualities of blueness and thereby to review, with refined vision, the ubiquitous presence of blue in our world. In the process he completely cuts across conventional categories of description (such as those which caused the critics originally to scorn Renoir's picture) and reorders the world according to radically different principles of association:

> She has been dead now nearly a century
> Who wears that blue of smoke curling
> Beyond a kiln, and blue of gentians,
> Blue of lazurite, turquoise hauled
>
> Over the blue waves.

Yet as the poem proceeds it is death that comes more and more to test (if not dominate) the canvass. Can this aesthetic of composition, so triumphantly vindicated by these intensely life-enhancing modalities of blue, successfully accommodate pain and suffering? Can an artifice of mutability indeed be found that will satisfactorily replace Yeats's artifice of eternity?

Fundamental to much of Ormond's poetry is the belief that art is a design against darkness (Frost's *momentary stay against confusion*), and that while such design has no foundation in reality it does correspond to the structure of human feeling and experience. A corollary of this is the paradox that art is most true to life when it is most itself, that is, precisely when in a sense it is most artificial. Temperamentally attracted to this view of art, Ormond found it natural to admire the intricate *cynghanedd* poetry of the Welsh masters of the middle ages. But he was equally naturally the product of modern Welsh culture, plain-speaking Nonconformist and almost aggressively egalitarian, tending to value the instantly accessible and communal. These two inclinations in his personal and artistic make-up manifested themselves in his poetry sometimes as two different styles of writing, sometimes as two clashing registers of speech (as already noted in 'Cathedral Builders'), and sometimes as two cross-fertilizing modes of expression. So, for instance, after producing in 'The Hall of Cynddylan' a vibrantly patterned English version of 'Ystafell Cynddylan', Ormond proceeded, in 'Landscape without Figures', to produce what is in part an anti-heroic modern commentary affecting to debunk the whole glamourizing arrangement of fine phrases: *There'd been some battle or other/ Fought in a bog, no doubt; as unromantic/ And merciless as ever.* However, he characteristically restores something of what he has just stripped away when he admits *The old poets were good at this kind of thing;/ A bit high-flown, but genuine enough;/ Cooking the metre but seldom the reaction.* That last phrase takes us to the paradoxical heart of the kind of conspicuous artistry practised by Ormond himself.

Rephrasing Matthew Arnold, Wallace Stevens made one of his most classic pronouncements:

The relation of art to life is of the first importance especially in a skeptical age, since, in the absence of a belief in God, the mind turns to its own creations and examines them, not alone from the aesthetic point of view, but for what they reveal, for what they validate and invalidate, for the support that they give.

For Ormond, too, art was a substitute for religion; hence the driven, obsessed quality of his attention to every verbal and graphic detail of his work. While being first and foremost a splendid portrait poem, 'The Piano Tuner' is also about precisely such a religious mania of artistic perfectionism; the Kafka-esque sense of living under mysterious judgement – if not of God then of *a language beyond us, . . . the quotients and ratios* of some undisclosed perfect artistic order. Blindness here becomes a terrifying metaphor for pure obliviousness to everything except the ruthless demands of one's artistic medium. *The house is not the same/ Until long after he leaves, having made one thing/ Perfect. 'Now play,' say his starched eyes.* The uneasy humour in the poem is testimony to its being a complex and unnerving exercise in self-knowledge, with Ormond acting the parts, as it were, of both the piano-tuner and the speaker.

But if religion is background to, and analogue for, Ormond's fascination with design, so are other areas of human experience, including the erotic. As its place in SELECTED POEMS shows, 'Certain Questions for Monsieur Renoir' is, in a sense, a love poem, the whole composition of paint in 'La Parisienne' being itself keyed to the sensual passion (both for person and for paint) that occasioned it: *The eyes are bells to blue/ Inanimate pigment set alight/ By gazing which was passionate./ So what is midnight to this midinette?* Ormond himself wryly admitted elsewhere that La Parisienne had not in fact been a seamstress, but that he had probably been seduced by the sensuous insinuations of meaning resulting from the juxtaposition of 'midinette' with 'midnight' – a perfect instance of the delinquent means art may find of telling a 'truth' . The erotic charge in 'Certain Questions' is reinforced, in SELECTED POEMS, by the placing of the poem next to 'Captive Unicorn', a poem which seems to be a distillation of the muted phallic sensuousness of a myriad medieval paintings on that subject. The poor mythical creature, rendered docile by *enchanter's nightshade*, domesticated, palisaded and bejewelled, dreams riotously yet impotently of *jack-by-the-hedge, lances/ Of goldenrod to crunch on, tangled/ Heart's ease, salads of nipple-wort.*

Introducing 'Design for a Quilt' on the radio, Ormond aptly referred to it as his *undress poem*, while claiming that

writing a love poem is like being given the freedom of a city, and the right to march up and down the streets of language with bayonets fixed, bands playing, and all in high ceremonial dress. One hasn't to fight the usual battle with language, to get meaning and the music of words in the right tension together.

The poem, he explained, had come from seeing,

in a New York museum, . . . an exhibition called 'The Twelve Masterpieces of American quilts'. And one of them had a great tree embroidered on it, but a tree with precious few leaves I thought – too few to keep the babes in the wood warm when they got lost again. But this thought stayed with me and became a prime image when I imagined a lover commissioning a present for his girl, and describing to the quilt-maker his design for a quilt.

The result, one might add, was an interesting modern contribution to, and variant of, a very old genre – the genre of the 'invitation' poem as most celebratedly practised by such poets as Marlowe ('Come live with me'), Donne ('To his Mistris on her going to bed') and Marvell, whose 'To his Coy Mistress' is of course a genially sardonic seduction poem. As, in a way, is 'Design for a Quilt' – the masculine speaker obviously has designs in self-delightingly weaving such a sumptuously pastoral setting for his pleasures. Hence the girl becomes, in several suggestive senses, *this object of designing* – some feminists might well object that she (like Donne's mistresses) is marginalized (virtually removed from the poem), reduced to an object of male desire, a figment of masculine fantasy. Be that as it may, the poem is clearly a modern, deliberately mannered, Metaphysical poem (compare the work of Bobi Jones or Richard Wilbur), even to its traditional *double entendres* and puns on 'falling', 'bearing' etc. And as with the Metaphysicals, what is being dramatized is the fusion of sense and of intellect which is a distinctive feature of the arousal of the human erotic imagination. Also as with the Metaphysicals what is being demonstrated is that there is an aesthetic, and a poetic, of the erotic – that sensuality can be a powerful motive for, and indeed a powerful element in, artistic 'designing'. (Indeed, the deep subject of the poem might be said to be its exposure of what it punningly calls *entwining motives*/[motifs].) Moreover, this sensuality is not confined, as it frequently is in Ormond's writing, to the realm of the aural and visual, but touchingly embraces the tactile. There is a palpable impression of body-warmth in many of the lines, as when the quilt is required to

> be warm enough that should she stir
> To draw a further foliage about her
> The encouraged shoots will quicken
> And, at her breathing, midnight's spring
> Can know new season as they thicken.

Through its decorous conceitedness such writing deliberately raises the issue of the equivocal relationship between art and nature, which was of course one of the great subjects of Renaissance art and poetry.

However, if this poem is Metaphysical in manner, it is so in a distinctively modern way, in that passion is here interwoven with protectiveness and considerate gentleness, and is infused with a sense of the reciprocities of affection that belong to a settled relationship. This 'seduction' is, after all, intended to result not only in pleasure but in procreation, just as the quilt is designed to be a future family heirloom: *she'll bequeath it/ To one or other of the line,/ Bearing her name or mine,/ With luck I'll help her make beneath it.* At that point the poem clearly blends in with Ormond's love poems to his wife, notably 'Cat's Cradles' which is printed alongside it in SELECTED POEMS. It takes courage, one commentator admiringly noted, to use the expression *serious popinjay* in a modern poem. But of course the phrase is wholly consonant with the elaborately teasing tone of verbal foreplay in a poem about the game of love and the interplay of feeling that are part of the constant ludic work of constructing a married relationship. Having originally intended a villanelle, Ormond told Richard Poole (*and if you look at it with that in mind, I think it will become pretty apparent – with the partial repetition of rhymes*) that he had then changed *to something more fluid, to give the hand-to-hand movement in the cat's cradle.* The lightness of rhythmic and verbal touch he achieves in this poem is of the essence, communicating as it does the way in which the substantialities of relationship are based on the subtlest patterns of evanescent exchange. And, of course, what the poem beautifully conveys is the sexuality that is at the heart of marriage. The domestic scene becomes the seat of a passion that is not thereby domesticated, as the lines enact the sly game of deferrals that heightens expectation and guarantees gratification. And in this poem which so nicely brings out the internal connections between home-making and making love, the key role is assigned to the woman, as the man (and poet), clumsy and previous, begins to *relay/ adroit reciprocations/ of design less than adroitly.*

'Cat's Cradles' is one of those fine poems by Ormond in which the rhythmic lineation seems to become the very lineament of breath. In this case it is the rocking rhythm and quickening pulse of passion that is caught, but in 'Summer Mist' it is the give and take of companionship that is celebrated through the figure of a summer tree's gently swaying branches that have *common tenancy/ Arrangements, moving in and out/ Of one another's air at the wind's/ Say-so.* Here there is a beautiful brief suspension of movement between one poetic line and the next, even as the meaning carries on and over, a delicate hesitation occasioned for instance by the juxtaposition of two words ('Wind's', 'Say-so') both of which are accentuated and both of which share a consonant (concluding and initial 's') that is nevertheless pronounced *differently* in the two respective cases ('z', 'ss'), so that a momentary effort of enunciation is required to distinguish one from the other. By such subtle methods is rhythm secretly determined and controlled – in this case a rhythm that creates the very sense of companionship with which the poem is concerned, namely that of living space held in common by two people, each of whom alternately occupies and vacates it. Elsewhere other rhythms are equally finely tuned to register other effects, as when in the haunting poem 'Homing Pigeons' Ormond creates sound-cluttered lines as jerkily unpredictable as the movement they describe: *Why then the falling, all the fumbling/ As tumbler pigeons, fools flying, with the most/ Inept of masteries?* It is almost a pastiche of Hopkins; a rendering of the instress of a random world entirely devoid of spiritual inscape.

V

Unable, as he was, to believe in any spiritual template for either life or art, Ormond instead looked for an alternative pattern of clarification, and found it very early in the natural cycle of growth and decay. In this respect his core vision changed very little in forty years. It was his misfortune as a writer to have been instinctively attracted and temperamentally suited to the very kind of cosmic vitalism which had in his day found definitive modern expression in the compacted poetry and organicist poetics of Dylan Thomas. That made his early 'natural' (in every sense) dependence on Dylan all the harder to break, and his independence of style as a poet all the harder to achieve. It is not surprising, either, that when he *did* evolve a style of his own that was authentically answerable to his sense of the dynamic processes of the natural cosmos, two of the best poems which he subsequently wrote on that subject should have been addressed to his artist friends, Ceri Richards and Graham Sutherland, whose neo-Romantic nature paintings carried an authoritative, distinctive, visual signature.

Ormond worked for so long on 'Salmon' that what he had originally intended as a gift for Ceri Richards turned into a commemoration of him. A meditative celebration of the salmon's blind natural compulsion to traverse unimaginable distances in order to spawn and die at the place of its beginning, the poem uses a repertoire of energizing devices to register the physical arduousness of such an epic adventure. Verbs are juicily unusual (*jounce over/ Shelves upstream*) or are repeatedly left clutching at space at the end of lines. Internal rhymes check the onward flow of language, just as the progress of the salmon is forcibly impeded: *They reach the churning wall/ Of the brute waterfall*. Adjectives and adverbs add a thickness of texture to things and movements (*The stream slides clear yet shirred/ With broken surface*). The fish are seen both as grimly effortful (*They lunge and strike*) and as transcendently graceful in their tensile muscularity: *The long past shoots them/ Into flight, out of their element./ In bright transilient sickle-blades/ Of light*. Those lines also reveal the way in which, throughout the poem, the salmon are seen in a double perspective, that of the acutely observant eye and that of the conceptualizing mind. In fact, as is first hinted in stanza three (with the apostrophizing of Heraclitus, the 'weeping philosopher') and fully confirmed at the close (with the appeal to Gautama, the Buddha), the whole piece is intended to function not only on a representational but also on a philosophical level. It is offered as vivid naked proof of the sexual dynamic of nature. As such the poem aims to convey the many aspects of that phenomenon, from the blind heedlessness of its processes, through the ruthless strength of the energies expended, to the wondrous alluring beauty, *the sensual music*, as Yeats put it, of *those dying generations*; it reminds us of *whatever is begotten, born and dies*. Ormond matches the sexual climax and slack anticlimax of the mating fish with his own verbal rapture and subsequent vagueness:

> seed laid on seed
> *In spunk of liquid silk.*

So in exhausted saraband their slack
Convulsions wind and wend galactic
Seed in seed, a found
World without end.

The male salmon's coming to climax is described as his reaching a *squanderous peak*, a phrase that seems precisely to characterize a key paradoxical feature of Ormond's own style of poetry, which is shown in his romantic attraction to an economy of verbal excess, his attempt to maintain an energizing balance between parsimony and profligacy of expression and his search for the maximum density of signification compatible with clarity of utterance. When he fails to control such a style (as he regularly did when young, and periodically did even in his maturity) his poetry becomes strained, turgid, convoluted. It is, indeed, no accident that one of his talismanic words is 'clenched'.

Even 'Salmon' has its limitations, as becomes apparent if it is compared with the quiet originality of such poems by Ted Hughes on related subjects as 'Salmon Eggs' and 'That Morning' (*Solemn to stand there in the pollen light/ Waist-deep in wild salmon swaying massed*), or with the manic quirkiness of Peter Redgrove's treatments of flux. But the poem does beautifully express what Ormond, when discussing Ceri Richards's work, called the *hunger for a balance between light and dark, the thrust of birth and descent into decay*. It offers appropriate homage to Richards's genius for capturing a world of prodigal metamorphosis, and for registering correspondences between processes – so the seed of the salmon seems naturally to suggest the *creamy stars// Of air*, a milky way. Ormond's poem to Graham Sutherland is necessarily very different, since it pays homage, again by way of sensitive stylistic imitation or re-presentation, to a very different painter; however, it also complements 'Salmon' in a way that alerts us to the fact that each of the poems isolates a key component of Ormond's imaginative make-up. 'Salmon' illustrates his passionate shaping response to the excitations of sense and to the currents of energy that galvanize the malleable creation. 'Landscape in Dyfed' proceeds from a deliberating analytical intelligence interested in scrupulously articulating the underlying architecture of forms and in comprehending the hidden logic of the visible. Thus Ormond imagines himself (like Sutherland) X-raying trees to their mysterious temporal core:

> *And in their limbs what compass of sun*
> *Is contained, what sealed apparitions of summer,*
> *What transfixed ambulations. If you could cut*
> *Right to the heart and uncouple the innermost rings*
> *Beyond those nerves you would see the structure of air.*

This imaginative act of dendrochronology shows us the mysticism of his profoundly reflective material-ism.

As those lines indicate, Ormond was interested in sending mental probes down through the strata of accumulated time. In 'Finding a Fossil' this becomes his means of imagining a kind of permanence. The straitened verse form and enfolded rhymes emblematize his own attempt to fossilize experience, to create *remembered shapes* that 'live' and to turn the greenness of present life into the compacted and salvific greyness of lasting stone. The Poundean image of the hewn voice of poetry no doubt held a particular appeal for a man who had spent so much of his life working in the then apparently ephemeral medium of film. Here the poem is in a sense about the very techniques it employs. It eloquently demonstrates that alliteration and assonance are preservatives; that out of *fragment and element* of language may be invented a means of reifying breath, of fixing the fleetingness of life's perishable movements: *A leaf preserved and pressed/ Between leaves of stone; crossed/ Rest and unrest.* It also highlights what might be called the Keatsian paradoxes of art – that luck is essential to the successful deployment of skill, that the warmth of life is best entrusted to the *cold stars* (of formal artistic pattern as well as of the cosmos) *that dance/ Gestures of permanence.*

It was of course the fossils discovered by early nineteenth-century geologists that ushered in a whole new post-Christian era based on a revolutionary scientific cosmogony. Specific, playful allusion is made to this at the end of 'Letter to a Geologist', a poem addressed to Ormond's lifelong friend Wynn Williams which nicely balances the geological against the human sense of time and both counterpoints and interweaves the languages of science and of poetry. Opening with an archaic poeticized passage full of the fabulous language of antique fable, the poem shows how the discoveries of geology can provide modern artists with an alternative, scientific discourse of wonder: *The shifting land you've shown me: off-shore/ Islands in green counties; tide-ways/ 500 million years of age under the plough.* As if recalling Donne's success in making Metaphysical poetry by remaking poetic metaphor in the image of the New Science, Ormond follows his reference to Sahara sand embedded in Deeside rock with the question: *If these could move, could not you move, too?* But the answer is 'no'. For human beings, Flintshire remains as stubbornly remote from Cardiff as the Seychelles are from Wales; human breathing does not move to the rhythm of continental drift. So Ormond's pressing invitation to Williams to visit, so that they can *tell/ Some part of earth's true time together* and *say to each other words of a common world*, is couched in nicely ambiguous language that embraces both the scientific and the contrastingly human sense of time. And in a way, in inviting him to sing *the lullabies you sang/ My children, come sing them again before sleep* Ormond is even quietly yet pointedly reinstating towards the end the apparently superannuated form of Romantic poetic expression burlesqued in the opening lines of his poem.

Come south, Ormond implores his friend: *Ferns in grey shale speak of you/ From my shelf, of coal measures we were both/ Born on.* In fact, Ormond's very early Dylanesque poem about his birth, which much later featured as the opening poem in REQUIEM AND CELEBRATION, was organized around the image of seams of fossil coal: *My husk began in a caged harvest,/ A river remembered light through ferns and leaves/ Set in stone by ancient summers.* It is therefore not surprising to find 'Letter to a Geologist' appearing in the Dunvant section of SELECTED POEMS. What is initially more puzzling is the inclusion of 'Paraphrase for Edwin Arlington Robinson' in that section. Then one realizes that it is both a Welsh portraitist's portrait of a notable American portraitist and a belated modern Romantic's tribute to one who himself penned a wry picture of his Romantic self in the guise of a Miniver Cheevy who *missed the medieval grace/ Of iron clothing*:

Miniver Cheevy, born too late,
Scratched his head and kept on thinking;
Miniver coughed, and called it fate,
And kept on drinking.

So, too, Ormond's blackly farcical paraphrase of Robinson's catastrophe-haunted life is in part a means of chronicling the disappointments to which any romantic temperament is heir:

It was Sod's Law and not the sun
That made things come unstuck for Icarus

The same applies to all with a seeming head
For heights, a taste for the high wires,

Flatulent aerialists who burped
At the critical moment then fell akimbo

The poem becomes a kind of *Bildungsroman* of the Romantic artist, and its particular relevance to Ormond's own case is underlined by the touching metaphor he undemonstratively makes of the hearing defect from which both he and Robinson suffered. Robinson is disabused of his belief that he has detected clues to some profound code when he discovers that the noises are simply *the eighth nerve/ Shrinking from lack of blood. That fenced you//High on a dangerous peak of vertigo, giddy/ But unfalling.* Ormond himself experienced the occasionally vertiginous sensation of risking the language of a high art which lacked the sanction, and safety-net, of either a secure reality principle or a foundational faith.

Ormond sees Robinson simultaneously as the elegist of *a lost Imperial music* and as the recorder of an incorrigibly diminished world:

a thin parish of prophets
Without words – except for baffled Amen,
A scraggy choir without a common hymn,

But no man without music in the throng
And each man sawing at his own bleak tune.

This may be read as an inverted compliment to the socially cohesive and spiritually harmonious Dunvant community which Ormond himself so nostalgically memorializes. Yet he does so in a Robinsonian spirit of baffled Amen, in the sense that, like Robinson, Ormond is permanently exiled from belief. His consequently ambiguous role as elegist of a community of believers is perhaps best seen in the masterly verbal and tonal equivocations of 'Right Time', a poem in memory of his grandfather, *That old man, who sang to me/ The hymns of all his certainties.* His grandfather's grandfather clock, with its gilt/guilt hands and *lost pulse, still stands still,* pointing to the once (and always?) right time of a now meaningless hour. There is always a danger that such a progressive allegorizing of the clock will result only in the multiplying of predictable puns at a tedious rate, but the poem avoids this, to a sufficient extent, through Ormond's skilled control of the tone of rueful rumination: *He and buried farms/ Talk to me through the fled arithmetic/ Behind these arbitrary numerals.*

What Ormond will not risk in portraying Dunvant, however, is the anti-sentimental bleakness of tone found in some of Robinson's strongest writing such as 'Richard Cory'. One sometimes yearns for the harsh accuracy, the cold douche, of the depiction of religious puritanism which is found in 'New England':

Passion is here a soilure of the wits,
We're told, and Love a cross for them to bear;
Joy shivers in the corner where she knits
And Conscience always has the rocking-chair.

Compared to that, Ormond's Dunvant sketches seem the victims of their own good nature, somewhat prone to sentimentality and lacking the cruel accuracy that makes for greatness in Lowell's ruthless New England portrait poetry of the late fifties and early sixties. Such comparisons are necessary, not only because Ormond actively invites them by placing the Robinson poem where he does but because disproportionate claims have been made for portrait poetry as a uniquely Welsh genre deriving from the supposedly laudable communal instincts of Welsh artists. It is tempting, although it would admittedly be too sweeping, to retort that all that is uniquely Welsh about the genre is the tendency for it to become a vehicle for sentimental hagiography or for whimsical anecdotalism in Welsh hands. Among prose writers, neither the Welsh-language D. J. Williams (whose elegiac memoirs mark the passing of a rural idyll) nor the English-language Gwyn Thomas (some of whose elegiac comedy exemplifies a corresponding, characteristic-ally Anglo-Welsh, form of industrial pastoralism) is immune from this weakness, and Ormond occasion-ally reminds one of both.

It could therefore be argued that some of the negative emotions he felt for Dunvant were displaced onto Robinson and found expression in his 'Paraphrase'. Where else in his mature poetry do we find even a hint of those feelings registered by him as a teenager in 1943 when coolly noting the plight of Enid, an 'imbecile', cared for by her neurotic mother, who *would be able to find much more happiness than she had now in the big, airy rooms supplied in Bridgend* [mental hospital]? Sharp-tongued though the older Ormond could reputedly be, kindliness is all in the Dunvant poems to an extent that is alternately touching and exasperating, and which may owe something to an underlying guilt incurred by the relative infrequency of his returns to his home village. So the portrait of a village 'imbecile' is softened into a whimsical picture of Johnny Randall, a sub-Wordsworthian 'idiot boy' who suffers from religious mania. The village drunk and colourfully black sheep, Wil Bando, is sent to his sad end in 'Full-Length Portrait of a Short Man', a poem in which gentleness tends towards indulgence as it also does in 'Organist'. In the latter the play on images relating to music ultimately becomes an irritatingly conspicuous stylistic tic. Perhaps the closest Ormond comes to a Robinsonian view of *the bad joke of the world* is in the picture of 'Froga', a mournful isolato, in appearance *Half frog, half ogre*, who is recalled as having *the eyes of a dying seal in a bankrupt circus*. But even here the poem is too neatly anecdotal in shape, and rather too pleased with its own clever effects. The perceived limitations of these altogether too fetching poems are worth stating so bluntly precisely because they are so eminently anthologizable in their simplicity and tend therefore to be substituted for work of appreciably higher quality. They appeal particularly to Welsh readers who, for reasons clearly deriving from the culture, mistrust all 'cleverness' in poetry, and who remind one of Wallace Stevens's wife. When asked what she thought of her husband's poetry, she replied, *I like Mr Stevens' poems when they are not affected. But they are so often affected.*

Choosing as he did to work within the constraints of the related modes of requiem and celebration, Ormond is at his best in such poems as 'After a Death', 'The Key', and 'My Grandfather and his Apple Tree'. It is appropriate that these should be among the strongest examples of his mature work, since from his earliest years as a writer his imaginative engagements with Dunvant had helped him develop a distinctive clarity of stylistic expression. This was true from the appearance of his first published poem, 'The Collier', to. that point sometime after 1950 when his father's death moved him to anticipate so many features of his later style in the superb family elegy, 'My Dusty Kinsfolk'. As early as 1946 he had published poems about his grandfather, mother and father respectively in THE WELSH REVIEW and he later included revised versions of them in REQUIEM AND CELEBRATION. While rather lush and fulsome in expression, these mannered products of his pseudo-Dylanesque period did have their moments of modest authenticity: *A collier's lamp lit the room she lived in./ The autumn leaves hung copper on the wall.* Nevertheless, their main usefulness today is as fixed reference points for estimating the full measure of his growth as an artist by the time he came to write the later emotionally complex elegy for his mother ('An Ending') and the gracefully terse, if slight, epitaphs on his father ('At his Father's Grave') and his uncle ('Epitaph for Uncle Johnnie').

The best Dunvant poems together amount to an anatomy of the experience of loss, including a sort of inventory of what has been taken away. After all, the Dunvant of his childhood and youth had virtually vanished by the time of his return to the area in the early fifties. Indeed, at the very time of his return, the EVENING POST, referring to the return of a native who sounds suspiciously like Ormond, noted his dismay at discovering that Dunvant had virtually been swallowed up in the insidious expansion of Swansea. In 'After a Death' (the title seems quietly to point up the contrast between this poem and Dylan Thomas's 'After the Funeral') the inventory of loss takes the form of registering the chill meagreness of what is left of, and after, a life, as Ormond notes the desultory detritus of abandoned things that have lost their former *raison d'être* as possessions. *White plates that write their O's across the dresser* seem to be saying not only that they are now O-rmond's but that in so being they are also nought. In a poem in which rhymes are movingly muted – many of them simply eye-rhymes, or off-rhymes, mere ghostly equivalences of sound – what seems most vivid and strong is *the slug's trail on the kitchen floor*. Ormond's ambiguous feelings about that interloping slug, which defaces yet hauntingly enlivens the deathly still scene, concentrate the unease that so powerfully pervades all the lines. In this Hardyesque poem the puns are particularly desolating – *the small effects of other people's lives* – and the phrases are beautifully disconsolate: *Pull back the curtains to let out the dark.* The words *A list's a list and offers me no order* turn this poem, which is so conspicuously marked by the futile attempt to order experience by listing words and objects, into a kind of elegy for elegy – a mourning for the unavailingness of mourning.

'The Key' revisits this experience as Ormond struggles, with his 'grandiose', unwieldy key, to recover the knack of gaining access to his old home. Ultimate success is, of course, attended only by failure: *The key/ Engages and the bolt gives to me/ Some walls enclosing furniture.* But in the attempt he elegizes a whole community and commemorates a vanished way of life fondly remembered for its proper pride in its working-class self, its strong spirit of mutuality and its habit of trust. The poem owes much of its power to the contrast between the bleakness of the concluding lines and the comfortableness of what has gone before, a comfortableness created by extensive anthropomorphism (the key and the lock are treated as old quarrelsome friends) and protective euphemism (*The others have gone for the long/ Night away*). Most of the poem is, therefore, a parable of what it means to feel at home. But then at the end a new reality breaks in, brutally registering itself as a new style. As *the bolt gives* it does not give the gift of home but simply allows the door to open on to *some walls* (the 'some' is masterly in its vagueness). And the melancholy of that anticlimax is reinforced by the special isolation of that last line, locked out, as it were, by the rhymes that make the preceding two lines a sealed couplet ('key'/'me').

A different level of loss is explored in 'My Grandfather and his Apple Tree', where the emphasis is on the losses incurred in the making of industrialized, chapel-ized south Wales. The poem has been neatly characterized by Tony Curtis as one that

works effectively at several levels; as an historical poem; as a family remembrance; it is an allegorical treatment of the life of a man as a social, economic and religious animal; the whole is a brilliantly sustained metaphor with a strong narrative structure. At its close one is left with the widowed miner brooding through his retirement years, regretting the lost sweetness of life, nettled around with sourness, devoid of juice.

Although it tends towards the stereotypical Anglo-Welsh image of Nonconformity, the poem is subtilized by Ormond's quizzical affection for an old man whose nature, he may have reluctantly sensed, in some ways resembled his own. There is the (guilty) sensuousness of the man, the tension between roistering freedom and responsibility, the love of light and growth, and the impulse to order by *untangl*[ing] *a brown garden into neat greens.* Yet when Ormond himself became a grandfather, recalling his own grandfather's dourness, he consciously sought to avoid replicating that character, and in the process discovered in his grandchildren a source of rejuvenation for himself both as man and as artist.

As Curtis shrewdly notes, 'My Grandfather and his Apple Tree' combines two kinds of poetry repeatedly favoured by Ormond; the narrative poem (where his talent for anecdote and the skills which he had acquired at PICTURE POST are much in evidence) and the parable-poem or poem of extended metaphor. Another of his favourite modes was the radial, or riddle, poem, so well described by Helen Vendler in an essay on Seamus Heaney (incidentally a poet with whom Ormond had made a short film and whose work he particularly admired):

The nature of adjectival poems is to be radial. All of Heaney's hazarding adjectival casts, radiating out from a central baffling subject, are the means of seeing facets too imaginatively overwhelming to be grasped as a whole. They are a way of encompassing perplexity, of encouraging the opaque into transparency.

96

No better example of such a procedure could be found than the following:

> *Not stitched to air or water but to both*
> *A veil hangs broken in concealing truth*

> *And flies in vague exactitude, a dove*
> *Born diving between rivers out of love*

> *In drums' crescendo beat its waters grow*
> *Conceding thunder's pianissimo*

> *Transfixing ancient time and legend where*
> *A future ghost streams in the present air:*

The answer to this riddle is, of course, a waterfall, and 'Definition of a Waterfall' illustrates the use which Ormond could make of both the traditional device of *dyfalu* (derived in part from Welsh-language strict-metre poetry) and a kind of writing that is intermediate between his early and his later styles, which is not wholly satisfactory, but which seems to be an attempt to mediate the one to the other. The poem as published was, in fact, the result of a reworking, in the mid-sixties, of a text first drafted in 1947.

However, it is the narrative style that again predominates in 'An Ending', the Dunvant poem which he chose to place in a section different from the others in SELECTED POEMS. That may be because he thought of this elegy for his mother as being set not so much in Dunvant as in limbo, that mental state which several of his late poems movingly instance. *Where else is there to sing/ Save where we are?* he asks in 'Where Else?', and other poems show him existing between past and present ('As it Happens'), surviving on an uneasy hedonism ('Among Friends') or awkwardly persisting ('Homing Pigeons'). There are many beautifully mellow affirmations of life's transience, its brief flaring appearance between dark and dark: in 'As it Happens' the word 'rejoiced' is made tellingly to rhyme with *having no choice*. That death, as Stevens famously put it, is the mother of beauty is the unspoken message of glorious passages like the following in 'Note from Cortona':

> *And each and cloudless morning I climb up*
> *By the broken flagstone path where the vines,*
> *Pleating the mountainside together, make slow*
> *Melodies on its patient staves; the sweet peas*
> *Gone, the blue moths' colour darkened*
> *Into the elder.*

The nagging yearning for the permanence of the transcendent is mocked in sub-Stevensonian style in 'For a Celestial Musician' and subjected to whimsical dismissal in 'Waiting in the Garden'. Yet it stubbornly recurs as a ground-note of regret or as a spice of melancholy in much of Ormond's writing. It is akin to what he calls in 'Elsewhere', *a branch's wraith of shadow on the ceiling*. And in the splendid 'Castiglion Fiorentino' – a poem that deserves, in spite of its feeble conclusion, to be set alongside Browning's minor 'Italian' masterpiece, 'Two in the Campagna' – such yearning is negatively present in the poignant rhythm of the mind's rueful adaptation to the serendipity and unrepeatability of experience. Returning to a spot that, through his long absence from it, has come to epitomize stillness and peace, Ormond anticipates

> *a prospect of calm*
> *That the heart hungers for and the heart*

Stops at, that is, if this is the place.

It is night, and there's no certainty.

Incidentally, it turned out to be the right place, he noted
in a broadcast. *But it wasn't quite the same. Turn your
back for eighteen years, let alone twenty, and what do the
Italians do? Build a football stadium slap in the middle of
the view.*

In so far as 'An Ending' is about living in
uncertainty, then, it is as much a Cortona poem as a
Dunvant poem. As he does elsewhere in 'Lazarus',
Ormond equivocatingly accepts the truth of
Wittgenstein's observation that since dying is the
final act and aspect of living, it can therefore offer us
no privileged insight into that ultimate otherness
which is death. But touching though his guilty,
almost grudging, scepticism is as he recalls his
mother's dying visions – of darkened chrysan-
themums, of friends beyond, of *dust on everything* –
the poem is marred by several false notes, most
evident in the shrill discords of the melodramatic
ending: *My lips upon your forehead tasted the foul grave/
And I spat it to my hand and rushed/ To wash the error
from my proud flesh.* Here the hysteria of disgust that
was probably the guilty experience which the poem
(first entitled 'Noli me tangere') was originally
written to expiate, continues to resist measured
expression.

Although he had *lost the reassurances of a formal faith,*
Ormond observed, *this doesn't mean that I don't
everyday wonder.* The remark, which clearly applies to
'An Ending', was one he actually made on radio
when introducing 'Ancient Monuments', his

monumentally fine poem about the mysterious power of *tall, pocked/ And pitted stones, grey, ochre-patched/ With moss, lodgings for lost spirits*. As Ormond went on to explain, the poem is appropriately dedicated to *Alexander Thom, the man who found the mathematical harmonies within the stone rings and alignments of standing stones, and tombs, the cromlechs of megalithic times*. Discovered by Ormond during the filming in the late sixties of A BRONZE MASK, the great cromlech at Gwâl y Filiast (which gave the poem its original title) awakened in him an abiding fascination. In the seventies, he returned to similar locations in the company of Professor Gwyn Williams, with whom he made two notable series of films about Welsh history from prehistoric times to the present. Williams's book of the series, THE LAND REMEMBERS, contains passages that provide an interesting gloss on 'Ancient Monuments', as well as on other poems such as 'Winter Rites' and 'Tricephalos'. There is, indeed, something residually filmic about the way this quest poem, 'Ancient Monuments', is itself constructed. The reader/ viewer is first specifically addressed (*You find them there . . .*) and then offered a series of visual images while a knowledgeable accompanying commentary instructs him or her in the secret history of this ancient land. But just as THE LAND REMEMBERS turns what originally was camera-work into guidebook instructions, so too does 'Ancient Monuments': *Turn and look back*, the reader is advised, and *You'll see horizons/ Much like the ones that they saw*. What is on view is, of course, much more than first meets the unsuspecting eye. The poem sets out to show how to read a landscape in depth, a process inseparable from learning how to read the poem itself in depth – learning, for example, to notice the doubleness of meaning hidden from the outset in such innocent phrases as *They bide their time* (the great standing stones patiently wait their chance/ they continue anciently to exist in their own mysteriously separate time-frame).

The power of the poem is probably due to Ormond's finding a perfect trope, in the stones' finally un-ascertainable place in the human and the natural landscapes, for his deep obsession as an artist with the insoluble enigma of death. Unlike 'Salmon' – the poem which succeeds it, and is thus made suggestively to contrast with it in SELECTED POEMS – 'Ancient Monuments' does not treat death simply as part of the cycle of nature. Indeed, the farmer's attempt to do so, by sowing *good grain/ To the tomb's doorstep*, is specifically seen as thwarted by the cromlech's inherent aloofness. Moreover, by imaging rampant fertility as a *chafing/ Loquacious thrust of seed/ This way and that*, and noting that it fails to overwhelm the stones, Ormond seems implicitly to be commenting on the futility of the human, poetic attempt to overcome the muteness of death through the garrulousness of language. There is something as moving as it is chilling about the way this poetry honestly contemplates the simple, blank cancellation by death of everything in which Ormond normally trusts and by which he passionately lives: colour, sound and movement. The poem ends with a meeting between an irresistible force and an infinitely re-movable, or removed, object:

> The racing barley, erratically-bleached
> Bronze, cross-hatched with gold
> And yellow, did not stop short its ride
> In deference. It was the barley's
> World. Some monuments move.

Here art (signified by the term 'cross-hatched') explicitly and almost defiantly declares its dependence upon and homage to the bounty of life. But if it is true that *it was the barley's world*, it is also true that *That tomb belonged in that field*: an inescapable fact for which art can ultimately offer no satisfactory redress.

'Ancient Monuments' deals, then, with the stillness that *is beyond decipherment*, and with whatever may exist *at the beginning and end of the heart's quandaries*. These phrases, though, come from 'Tuscan Cypresses', Ormond's other outstanding poem on the same topic, and the supreme example of his use of what Vendler called 'radial form.' This, the longest and the richest poem in his mature *oeuvre*, is structured around multiple exploration (through a succession of definitions) of a single nodal phenomenon that remains irreducibly unknowable but inexhaustibly significant. Each attempt at figurative or conceptual definition of the cypresses is self-cancelling, and thus draws attention to its own provisionality, or approximateness, as meaning. In this sense, the whole poem is about the poet's metrical and metaphorical *improvisations* compared to the *strict measure* of the trees. But if the cypresses are the negation of art (*They are the silences between the notes Scarlatti left unwritten,/ The silence after the last of Cimarosa's fall*), they are also of course its perpetual *fons et origo*, what Wallace Stevens would call *the motive for metaphor*. Art is thus again seen as the modern successor of religion, and in places the poem deliberately resembles a secular hymn or psalm.

Those references to Scarlatti and Cimarosa retrospectively affect the opening lines of the poem, adding a musical connotation to the spatial denotation of the word 'intervals': *Black-green, green-black, unbending intervals/ On far farm boundaries.* Already at this point words are being conspicuously forced to serve a double purpose ('black-green, green-black', 'intervals', etc.), to equivocate fruitlessly in an attempt to define the very essence of the cypresses. Indeed, the whole poem is about a 'boundary' experience, and is thus connected to many others by Ormond on the same theme. The most obvious of these, of course, is the poem 'Boundaries' itself, a poem (knowingly written in one of the greatest Romantic traditions – who could read such a work without recalling Shelley's 'To a Skylark' and countless others?) which beautifully illumines the fact that, as Edmund Burke famously put it, art *is* man's nature. Man can never step over *into* nature, being instead *trapped inside what he whistles* in a sense very different from a bird. So the cypresses are *beyond decipherment* – their meaning in themselves (intuited as a secret code) is not susceptible of being determined by translation into the human code of language and of art.

The stance of the cypresses *seems set as though by ordinance and yet it is not./ It is merely the circumstance of the mystery, the reason for churches.* A religious poem of sorts (like so much of Ormond's work), 'Tuscan Cypresses' deserves to be set alongside Waldo Williams's celebrated 'Mewn Dau Gae' ('In Two Fields') as an outstanding example of the apocalyptic strain in the modern Welsh imagination. But unlike Williams, of course, Ormond takes a non-Christian view of the end of all things in utter annihilation – *since it all comes to nothing./ See how it all burns, all, in the black flames of their silence, their silence, untelling*. Both in his vision, and in the language he fashions for expressing it, Ormond shares with Waldo Williams, though, an immense debt, consciously acknowledged, to the great English Romantics of both the nineteenth and the twentieth centuries. For instance, the very title of his poem places it in suggestive relationship with the opening of D. H. Lawrence's 'Cypresses' – an example of how in his later (as opposed to his earlier) work Ormond could be creatively indebted without being derivative (and could indeed deliberately deal in intertextuality, as he himself once pointed out when indicating the presence of poems by Hardy and Graves behind his own 'shaving poem', 'As it Happens'):

> *Tuscan cypresses,*
> *What is it?*
>
> *Folded in like a dark thought*
> *For which the language is lost,*
> *Tuscan cypresses,*
> *Is there a great secret?*
> *Are our words no good?*

Beginning thus, Lawrence's poem develops into a brooding meditation on the ancient Etruscans, whereas Ormond's moves in an altogether different direction, developing in the process a mode of apprehension more reminiscent of another famously death-haunted Romantic who is eventually named: [The trees] *are at the heart/ Of the ultimate music; the poor loam and Roman melody of Keats's body/ Sings silently beneath them*. It also sings silently beneath many of the lines of 'Tuscan Cypresses', reminding us that for so many of the great English Romantic poets, Italy was, as it was intermittently for Ormond, in Byron's celebrated phrase, *that paradise of exiles*. Arguably Ormond's supreme achievement, 'Tuscan Cypresses' is a modern Romantic poem not altogether unworthy of being placed alongside the poetry of the great Romantics themselves.

VI

Although much has understandably been made of John Ormond's craftsmanship, it is a term that needs careful handling. *I have always tried*, Lawrence explained in a letter to his friend Edward Marsh, *to get an emotion out in its own course, without altering it. It needs the finest instinct imaginable, much finer than the skill of craftsmen . . . Remember, skilled poetry is dead in fifty years*. It is a valuable reminder that for a poet the concept of craftsmanship, admittedly central though it has been to the Welsh poetic tradition, may be as much of a disabling as an enabling ideal. This is a particular danger when, as may partly have been the case with John Ormond, a Welsh poet is inclined to feel provincial and so is tempted to overcompensate by cultivating what is in fact a rather conventional sense of refinement. If in one sense Ormond's early struggle was to make his Romanticism potent and contemporary, his later effort was to avoid making his poetry no more than impressively accomplished after a somewhat conservative fashion – his fondness for what could sometimes be a rather predictable, though intricate, kind of verbal music being one potential area of weakness. Related to this was the problem, particularly acute for one whom Glyn Jones kindly and perceptively described as a natural aesthete, of developing an aesthetic that could deal with the rough as well as the smooth of things. In addition, Ormond was prone to lapses in tone (several of his love poems suffer from mawkishness, as Robert Minhinnick has noted), he did sometimes over-elaborate (even 'Certain Questions for Monsieur Renoir' might profitably be shorter than it is), he could relax into mere whimsy ('Night in a Hundred'), could be windily rhapsodic ('To a Nun'), and occasionally he took refuge in burnished cliché (*with creaking baskets laden*).

But such a litany of shortcomings is as misleading as it is ungracious, since Ormond at his notable best succeeded in practising a very special and valuable kind of craft – the subtle craft of a verbal equilibrist, to borrow a term from John Crowe Ransom, a twentieth-century poet whom Ormond periodically resembles. He was one for whom poetry was a means of striking a difficult balance between such destructively simplistic alternatives as life and artifice, belief and unbelief, stylistic plainness and obscurity. Moreover, like many another artist, Ormond found that only in and through art could such a complex equilibrium be maintained. Otherwise he remained a man at odds with himself in many ways, torn not least between his many talents (including his zestful talent for company). He had further to struggle with the want, in Wales, of a culture multifaceted enough to accommodate, let alone advance, his particular combination of abilities – a problem, one suspects, that hampered the development of other like spirits, such as his close friend Glyn Jones. The resulting tension of creative dissatisfaction in him manifested itself in many ways: as an innovative restlessness of mind, a hospitable generosity of imagination, an impressive omnivorousness of interest, an enlivening unpredictability of reaction and an occasional profligacy of unfocused energy. It could also sometimes be manifested as arrogance, irritability and touchiness, as Tony Conran sympathetically suggested in the opening section of the gift poem, 'Borage', which he wrote in honour of John Ormond:

An uncomfortable plant –
It lolls about,
Every part of it prickly
Like a hair shirt

However, after paying a nice compliment to 'Certain Questions for Monsieur Renoir' by imitating that poem's impassioned paean to blueness, Conran finds in borage a symbol of what he most values about Ormond the poet:

An uncomfortable plant –
Fit emblem for those
Poets in an age of tidy
And calamitous prose
Who have the ungainliness
Of a personal gait –
One might call it the penalty
Of being human too late.
Poets who know the unillusioned gaze
And mantle that vision
With the claws of the wild beast,
The human condition.
And now and then, making no show
Opening out
Into that perfection of blue
From one or two shoots –
Blue that one can sometimes see
In the eyes of first love,
The certificated blue
No falsehood can have . . .

It is a perceptive tribute by an eminent fellow poet and critic, a considered judgement that as both poet and film-maker John Ormond was indeed an originating artist of genuine integrity, humane vision and highly distinctive achievement. Blessed, but also burdened, with a diversity of talents, he could fulfil himself only by variously striving to do justice to them all. And it was under these demanding conditions that he succeeded in producing a valuable body of work, still vivified by the sense of wonder of one who loved, and lived by, Christopher Fry's suggestive maxim that *poetry is the language in which man explores his own amazement.*

Select Bibliography

A full bibliography can be found in John Harris (ed.), A BIBLIOGRAPHICAL GUIDE TO TWENTY-FOUR MODERN ANGLO-WELSH WRITERS. Cardiff: University of Wales Press, 1994.

JOHN ORMOND

Books, and books edited

INDICATIONS. London: Grey Walls Press, 1943. Poems by John Ormond Thomas, James Kirkup and John Bayliss.

REQUIEM AND CELEBRATION. Swansea: Christopher Davies, 1969.

DEFINITION OF A WATERFALL. London: Oxford University Press, 1973.

PENGUIN MODERN POETS 27: JOHN ORMOND, EMYR HUMPHREYS, JOHN TRIPP. Harmondsworth: Penguin, 1979.

GRAHAM SUTHERLAND, O.M.: A MEMORIAL ADDRESS: ANERCHIAD COFFA: DISCORSO COMMEMORATIVO: ÉLOGE FUNÈBRE. Cardiff: National Museum of Wales, 1981. (Text of an address delivered at the Mass of Thanksgiving for the artist's life, Westminster Cathedral, 29 April 1980.)

IN PLACE OF EMPTY HEAVEN: THE POETRY OF WALLACE STEVENS. Swansea: University College of Swansea, 1983. (W. D. Thomas Memorial Lecture.)

SELECTED POEMS. Bridgend: Poetry Wales Press, 1987.

JOHN TRIPP: SELECTED POEMS, edited by John Ormond. Bridgend: Seren Books, 1989.

CATHEDRAL BUILDERS AND OTHER POEMS; with drawings by the author. Newtown: Gwasg Gregynog, 1991.

Selected contributions to books and periodicals

'Borrowed Pasture: Notes on a Film', JOURNAL OF FILM AND TELEVISION ARTS (Summer 1961), 6–8.

'Horizons hung in air: Kyffin Williams', LONDON WELSHMAN (November 1966), 7–9. Transcript of BBC Wales TV interview by John Ormond.

'A music restored', PLANET 7 (1971), 75–7. Review of Glyn Jones, SELECTED SHORT STORIES.

'R. S. Thomas, priest and poet: A transcript of John Ormond's film for BBC Television, broadcast on April 2, 1972; introduced by Sam Adams', POETRY WALES 7:4 (1972), 47–57.

'Ceri Richards: Root and branch', PLANET 10 (1972), 3–11.

'Ceri Richards', in ARDDANGOSFA GOFFA CERI RICHARDS 1973: CERI RICHARDS MEMORIAL EXHIBITION 1973. Cardiff: National Museum of Wales, 1973, 7–11.

Autobiographical essay, in Meic Stephens (ed.), ARTISTS IN WALES 2. Llandysul: Gwasg Gomer, 1973, 155–64.

'John Ormond writes', in Dannie Abse (ed.), CORGI MODERN POETS IN FOCUS 5. London: Corgi, 1973, 133–5.

'Gwyn Thomas', in James Vinson (ed.), CONTEMPORARY NOVELISTS OF THE ENGLISH LANGUAGE. London: St James's Press, 1976, 1360–2.

'In certain lights: Extracts from a work in progress', PLANET 36 (1977), 37–39.

'An ABC of Dannie Abse', in Joseph Cohen (ed.), THE POETRY OF DANNIE ABSE. London: Robson, 1983, 108–35.

'There you are, he's an artist', in CERI RICHARDS: AN EXHIBITION TO INAUGURATE THE CERI RICHARDS GALLERY, THE TALIESIN CENTRE, UNIVERSITY COLLEGE, SWANSEA. Swansea: University College of Swansea, 1984, 22–4.

'Introduction', in KYFFIN WILLIAMS R.A.: A CATALOGUE FOR A RETROSPECTIVE EXHIBITION/ CATALOG AR GYFER ARDDANGOSFA ADOLYGOL. Cardiff: National Museum of Wales, 1987, 10–27.

'Picturegoers' (1980), and SELECTED POEMS (1987), in Patrick Hannan (ed.), WALES ON THE WIRELESS: A BROADCASTING ANTHOLOGY. Llandysul: Gomer, 1988, 58–60; 166–8.

'Letter from Tuscany', POETRY WALES 24:1 (1988), 20–4.

'Beginnings', in Patrick Hannan (ed.), WALES IN VISION. Llandysul: Gomer, 1990, 1–10.

Television films

A SORT OF WELCOME TO SPRING. Reading by Meredith Edwards of poems selected by John Ormond (1958/1960).

BORROWED PASTURE. A portrait of two Polish ex-servicemen farming in Carmarthenshire (1960).

ONCE THERE WAS A TIME. Documentary portrait of past life in the Rhondda, centring on the talk of two old colliers (1961).

Y GYMRU BELL: TAITH I BATAGONIA. The Welsh in Patagonia (1962).

THE DESERT AND THE DREAM. The Welsh in Patagonia (1962).

FROM A TOWN IN TUSCANY. Portrait of Arezzo centring on the town choir's preparations to visit Llangollen International Eisteddfod (1963).

RETURN JOURNEY: THE STORY OF [DYLAN THOMAS'S] RETURN JOURNEY TO SWANSEA (1964).

SONGS IN A STRANGE LAND. A study of the cosmopolitan religious culture of Cardiff's dockland (1964).

THE MORMONS (1965).

TROUBLED WATERS: HARRY SOAN INVESTIGATES A CRISIS ON OUR RIVERS (1965).

MY TIME AGAIN: RICHARD BURTON (1965).

JUST LOOK AGAIN (1966).

UNDER A BRIGHT HEAVEN: A FILM PORTRAIT OF VERNON WATKINS (1966).

HORIZONS HUNG IN AIR: AN IMPRESSION OF KYFFIN WILLIAMS, PAINTER, AND OF HIS WORK (1966).

MUSIC IN MIDSUMMER. Film on Llangollen International Eisteddfod (1968).

A BRONZE MASK: A FILM IN ELEGY FOR DYLAN THOMAS (1969).

THE FRAGILE UNIVERSE: A PORTRAIT OF ALUN LEWIS, POET AND SOLDIER (1969).

THE ANCIENT KINGDOMS: A VIEW OF WALES. A film to mark the Prince of Wales's investiture: music by Daniel Jones (1969).

PIANO WITH MANY STRINGS: THE ART OF CERI RICHARDS (1969).

PRIVATE VIEW OF ART AND ARTISTS IN WALES: LESLIE NORRIS (1970).

ROBERT GRAVES (1970).

THE LAND REMEMBERS. 'A series in which Gwyn Williams travels the length and breadth of Wales . . . a personal account of Welsh archaeology and history' (1972).

R. S. THOMAS: PRIEST AND POET (1971/72).

THE LAND REMEMBERS (second series) (1974).

A DAY ELEVEN YEARS LONG. Film portrait of the painter, Josef Herman (1975).

ONE MAN IN HIS TIME: THE WORLD OF W. J. G. BEYNON, FRS (1975).

Y TEITHWYR. On the artist John 'Warwick' Smith, set in 1797 (1976).

SUTHERLAND IN WALES (1977).

FORTISSIMO JONES (a portrait of the composer, Daniel Jones) (1977).

THE LIFE AND DEATH OF PICTURE POST (1977).

A LAND AGAINST THE LIGHT. A portrait of the painter, Kyffin Williams (1978).

THE COLLIERS' CRUSADE. South Wales miners and the International Brigade in the Spanish Civil War (1979).

POEMS IN THEIR PLACE (1980).

Selection of contributions to radio

A portrait of Frances Richards, wife of the artist Ceri Richards. Radio Wales and network, 13 & 25 February 1980.

'The voice of Meadow Prospect: A radio portrait of the prolific writer and storyteller, Gwyn Thomas', Network Radio 4, 29 September 1981.

'John Ormond introduces and reads a selection from his recent work – poems of love and the cosmic context in which it is set', in the series THE LIVING POET, Radio 3, 22 January 1982.

'Apples from a rose bush: An assessment of the work of the author and poet, Glyn Jones', Radio 4, 29 September 1982.

Publications about John Ormond

Abse, Dannie. Introduction, in D. Abse (ed.), CORGI MODERN POETS IN FOCUS 5. London: Corgi, 1973, 127–33.

——'John Ormond as portraitist', POETRY WALES 26:2 (1990), 5–7.

Berry, David. WALES AND CINEMA: THE FIRST HUNDRED YEARS. Cardiff: University of Wales Press, 1994, 290–7.

Berry, Ron. 'What comes after?', POETRY WALES 27:3 (1991), 54–5.

Brown, Tony. 'At the utmost edge: The poetry of John Ormond', POETRY WALES 27:3 (1991), 31–6.

Collins, Michael J. 'The Anglo-Welsh poet John Ormond', WORLD LITERATURE TODAY 51 (1977), 534–7.

——'Craftsmanship as meaning: The poetry of John Ormond', POETRY WALES 16:2 (1980), 25–33.

——'John Ormond', in Vincent B. Sherry (ed.), POETS OF GREAT BRITAIN AND IRELAND, 1945–1960. Detroit: Gale, 1984. Dictionary of Literary Biography: 27, 269–75.

——'The elegiac tradition in contemporary Anglo-Welsh poetry', ANGLO-WELSH REVIEW 76 (1984), 46–57.

——'The gift of John Ormond', POETRY WALES 27:3 (1991), 4–8.

Curtis, Tony. 'Grafting the sour to sweetness: Anglo-Welsh poetry in the last twenty-five years', in Tony Curtis (ed.), WALES THE IMAGINED NATION: STUDIES IN CULTURAL AND NATIONAL IDENTITY. Bridgend: Poetry Wales Press, 1986, 99–126.

Hooker, Jeremy. 'The accessible song: A study of John Ormond's recent poetry', ANGLO-WELSH REVIEW 23: 51 (1974), 5–12. Reprinted in Hooker, THE PRESENCE OF THE PAST: ESSAYS ON MODERN BRITISH AND AMERICAN POETRY. Bridgend: Poetry Wales Press, 1987, 107–13.

Jenkins, Randal. 'The poetry of John Ormond', POETRY WALES 8:1 (1972), 17–28.

Jones, Glyn. 'John Ormond: 1923–1990', POETRY WALES 26:2 (1990), 3–5.

Minhinnick, Robert. 'The echo of once being there: A reflection on the imagery of John Ormond', POETRY WALES 27:3 (1991), 51–3.

Norris, Leslie. Review article on REQUIEM AND CELEBRATION, POETRY WALES 5 (1969), 47–53.

O'Neill, Chris. 'Notes towards a bibliography of John Ormond's works', POETRY WALES 16:2 (1980), 34–8.

Ormond, Glenys. ' "J.O." and "Rod" ', POETRY WALES 27:3 (1991), 24–45.

Poole, Richard. 'The voices of John Ormond', POETRY WALES 16:2 (1980), 12–24.

——Review of SELECTED POEMS, POETRY WALES 23:1 (1988), 62–4.

——'Conversation with John Ormond', NEW WELSH REVIEW 2:1 [5] (1989), 38–46.

——'John Ormond and Wallace Stevens: Six variations on a double theme', POETRY WALES 27:3 (1991), 16–26.

Smith, Dai. 'A cannon off the cush', ARCADE (14 November 1980), 13–14.

——'John Ormond, first hand', RADIO WALES (1990). A programme in memory of John Ormond.

Stephens, Meic. 'From Picture Post to Poetry', obituary in the GUARDIAN (9 June 1990).

Tripp, John. 'John Ormond', in James Vinson (ed.), CONTEMPORARY POETS OF THE ENGLISH LANGUAGE. 2nd ed., London: St James's Press, 1976, 1153–5.

The Author

M. Wynn Thomas, a native of Ferndale (Rhondda) and Penyrheol (Gorseinon), is professor of English at the University of Wales, Swansea, and a former chair of the Welsh Arts Council's Literature Committee. He is the author or editor of more than a dozen books in the fields of American poetry, Welsh writing in English, and Welsh-language literature, including INTERNAL DIFFERENCE: TWENTIETH-CENTURY WRITING IN WALES (1992). His MORGAN LLWYD: EI GYFEILLION A'I GYFNOD (1991) was awarded a Welsh Arts Council prize, while the publication of THE LUNAR LIGHT OF WHITMAN'S POETRY (1987) led to two periods as visiting professor at Harvard University. His most recent publications include DIFFINIO DWY LENYDDIAETH CYMRU (1995), and DAIL GLASWELLT (1995), a translation into Welsh of selections from Walt Whitman's LEAVES OF GRASS. In 1996, Professor Thomas was made vice-chair of Yr Academi Gymreig and was elected a Fellow of the British Academy.

Designed by Jeff Clements
Typesetting at the University of Wales Press in
11pt Palatino and printed in Great Britain by
Dinefwr Press, Llandybïe, 1997

British Library Cataloguing in Publication Data.
A catalogue record for this book is available from the
British Library.

ISBN 0-7083-1406-6

The Publishers wish to acknowledge the financial
assistance of the Arts Council of Wales towards the cost
of producing this volume.